# The Little Book of Value Investing

Christopher H. Browne
Foreword by Roger Lowenstein

**16**

EasyRead Large

RHYW

# Copyright Page from the Original Book

# TABLE OF CONTENTS

# More Praise for The Little Book of Value Investing

"A lot of wisdom in a little book. This is an essential read for any investor of any size. It lays out the basics of value investing in a clear and lucid primer. I am assigning it as homework to all of our shareholders!"
Charles M. Royce, President, The Royce Funds

"Value investors want a lot for their money. Chris Browne explains why—and how to do it. This short and enjoyable book gives investors lots of value for the time they invest."
Charles D. Ellis, Author, *Capital*

"Chris Browne is one of the giants in the field of global value investing. Well worth reading!"
Martin J. Whitman, Third Avenue Funds

"Chris Browne is an outstanding practitioner of wealth creation."
Bruce Greenwald, Columbia Business School

"Chris Browne provides an engaging exposé on the principles and processes that have made him an industry legend. A must read for investors of any persuasion and experience."

Lewis Sanders, Chairman and CEO, Alliance Bernstein

# Little Book Big Profits Series

In the *Little Book Big Profits* series, the brightest icons in the financial world write on topics that range from tried-and-true investment strategies we've come to appreciate to tomorrow's new trends.

Books in the *Little Book Big Profits* series include:

*The Little Book That Beats the Market,* where Joel Greenblatt, founder and managing partner at Gotham Capital, reveals a "magic formula" that is easy to use and makes buying good companies at bargain prices automatic, enabling you to successfully beat the market and professional managers by a wide margin.

*The Little Book of Value Investing,* where Christopher Browne, managing director of Tweedy, Browne Company, LLC, the oldest value investing firm on Wall Street, simply and succinctly explains how value investing, one of the most effective investment strategies ever created, works, and shows you how it can be applied globally.

*The Little Book of Index Investing,* where Vanguard Group Founder John C. Bogle shares his own time-tested philosophies, lessons, and personal anecdotes to explain why outperforming the market is an investor illusion, and how the simplest of investment strategies—indexing—can deliver the greatest return to the greatest number of investors.

# Foreword

My first stock—Poloron Products—was a clinker. My father bought 400 shares for me in the early 1960s. I never knew what it made or what it did. But I adopted the custom of checking the price each morning. (In the technologically distant era of my youth, believe it or not, people still relied on the newspaper to discover what the market had done the previous day.) It amazed me that an advance of merely 1/8 would enrich me by $50, a prodigious sum. The stock went down as often as it went up, but I tended to disregard the declines—it was only paper, right?—while experiencing a momentary thrill on the advances. I remember asking my father what caused the stock to go up. His answer made sense, but only up to a certain point. Poloron was in business—that much I understood. And the more profitable the business, the more that people would pay for the stock. But—and here was the rock on which my comprehension foundered—the profits didn't "go" to the stock. They went to the company. The quotations I perused in the morning *Times* had no direct link—of this much I was sure—to the revenue that materialized in the company's coffers. So why did the shares advance? My father said something about the profits conferring on the company the *ability* to pay the shareholders dividends. But here again, Poloron's discretion seemed complete. They did not have to pay us, the shareholders, each of whom I imagined to be a lad much like myself, anything at all. We were at their mercy. That the price (or so my father said) responded faithfully to the developments in the business, I ascribed to the peculiar character of the stock market. I understood it, if at all, as a sort of cheering section knit by a ritualized set of financial rules. The mysterious people who determined the price of my 400 shares were apparently honor-bound to do so in accordance with the outlook for Poloron's profits, regardless of the fact that I and the other stockholders might never see them.

I do not remember my father ever telling me he sold the stock, but one day he must have done so. I seemed to know that the 400 shares were no longer *my* 400 and Poloron ceased to be my concern. Still, it left me with a certain mind-set. I did not earn a profit, but I gained a habit that, when I started writing about, as well as buying, stocks, turned out to be ingrained.

Wall Street teaches, variously, that stocks are driven by all manner of concerns—by war and peace, by politics, by economics, by the market trend, and so forth. My inheritance was a credo: Stocks are driven by the underlying earnings.

I thought about this while reading Christopher Browne's estimable synopsis of value investing. It is a cliché that, when it comes to rooting for a sports team, we inherit the passions of our fathers. It is similarly true that our parents' economic prejudices also mold our own. Our first financial instructions are those we hear from our folks, most usually the family wage-earner (in my generation, the dad). We hear them with young, impressionable ears and a lifetime is insufficient to shake them.

In Browne's case, this was all to the good. He gives, here, just a modest hint of his financial blood lines. His father, Howard Browne, was a stockbroker who, in 1945, helped to found Tweedy, Browne and Reilly, the firm where the author has long been a principal. To call the founding generation "brokers" is a gross generalization. They were Wall Street specialists of a peculiar ken, who put together buyers and sellers of shares in small, thinly traded securities for which no broad market existed. By definition, then, their customers were those who were drawn to the underlying value of a stock as distinct from the market trend—with respect to these stocks, remember, there *was* no active market. Indeed, one of the firm's early and most active clients was Benjamin Graham, the pioneering professor, financial writer, and money manager.

Graham essentially created the discipline of value investing, and his disciples became its first practitioners. Among this small but devoted tribe,

Tweedy, Browne was immediately established as virtually hallowed ground. The firm took office at 52 Wall Street, down the hall from Graham himself (the better to get his business and, presumably, his counsel). It eventually expanded from brokerage into money management—that is, to investing—in which it naturally employed Graham's approach.

Value investing is easy to describe, even if it is not always easy to execute in practice. It consists of buying securities for less than their intrinsic worth—of buying them on the basis of their underlying *business* value, as distinct from what is happening at the superficial level of the stock market. (Remember those mysterious fellows who bid up Poloron's stock on the basis of its earnings? They were onto something.)

Since the game is about price and value—that is, paying less than what you are getting—it is not surprising that value investors tend toward beaten-down securities whose prices have been falling. They are the mirror image of momentum investors, who get excited as prices rise. As Christopher Browne explains, "Buy stocks as you would groceries—when they are on sale."

But we are not quite finished with the father. One of the stocks the older Browne dealt in was a beaten-down textile manufacturer in New England, Berkshire Hathaway Inc. Graham nearly bought it in the late 1950s but decided to pass. But one of his young associates and former pupils at Columbia Business School, Warren Buffett, took an interest in Berkshire. And as textiles were having their troubles, the stock kept getting cheaper.

By the early 1960s, Graham had retired and Buffett had his own firm. And Buffett, as we now know, did buy Berkshire. According to the younger Browne, it was his father, in his brokerage capacity at Tweedy, Browne, who bought "most of the Berkshire Hathaway that Buffett owns today." Few stocks have ever turned out better. Buffett started buying Berkshire at less than 8. When he cashiered the management, a few years later, and started to remake the company, it had risen to 18. Today, each share of Berkshire fetches $90,000. The Browne lineage thus connects directly to Buffett as well as to his teacher, Graham. In value investing, you cannot do better.

One of the curiosities of value investing, given the successful examples of Graham, Buffett, and numerous of their disciples, including Tweedy, Browne, is why the discipline is practiced so infrequently. What is it that stops investors from adopting methods that have consistently worked for over seven decades? Investors are nothing if not anxious, and in this case, I suspect their anxiety has something to do with the question I wrestled with as regards my earliest investment. Say that a stock is cheap: How does one know that it will not remain so? Why, in other words, should earnings at the corporate level drive the price in what is, after all, a secondary market for traded shares? J. William Fulbright, a U.S. senator, actually put the question to Graham during the mid-1950s, when Graham was testifying on the market. "It is mystery to me as well as to everybody else," Graham admitted. "We know from experience that eventually the market catches up with value."

The issue is taken up at length in the present volume and, as you will see, it is a mystery no longer. A whole industry exists of folks (including the author) who continuously assess what stocks are worth, based on their sales, profits, cash flow, and other business indicators. Let a stock linger at too much of a discount and some sharp-eyed operator will attempt to acquire it, based on the same calculation of profit. The business value thus acts (over time) as a floor beneath the stock price—it is what gives value investors such confidence.

Why, then, is value investing *still* so unconventional? Browne suspects it is a question of temperament. Given the vagaries of markets, he does not know—he *cannot* know—whether it will take a week, a month, a year, or even longer for the value in a stock to be recognized. Many people do not have the patience; they are eager for instant gratification, or for validation from their peers.

We need not dwell on the point, for it is the hesitation of the many that creates the opportunity for the few. For those do who have the temperament, the profits will be validation enough. This book is one of the very few that will give you the tools. The rest, dear reader, is up to you.

ROGER LOWENSTEIN

# Acknowledgments

I am greatful to the mentors, colleagues, and friends in the value investing community who have shaped my thinking and my career over the past 37 years. My journey began in June 1969 when I walked into the offices of Tweedy, Browne, and Knapp to borrow $5 from my father for a train ticket home. It was there that I met my father's partner Ed Anderson who proceeded to give me an introductory course in value investing and ended up hiring me for the summer. I haven't left yet. A physicist by training, Ed caught the investing bug while working for the Atomic Energy Commission in the 1950s and 1960s. Ed indoctrinated me into the ways of value investing.

Early thanks also go to Tom Knapp and my father, who gave me the freedom to explore new investment opportunities and practice stock picking at a very early age. I have been especially fortunate to have had two partners for nearly 30 years, John Spears and my brother Will Browne.

The success of our firm has been built on a foundation of shared trust and mutual respect. Thanks also to Bob Wyckoff and Tom Shrager, our two newer partners who nevertheless have been with us for more than 15 years each. Somehow the culture of humility and integrity that started with Ed, Tom, and my father has been transferred to the next generation. Rare is the partnership that has stood the test of so many years without any clash of egos.

We also have some of the brightest analysts in the business, which makes our job of being successful value managers much easier. I like to think of Tweedy as the Vatican City of value investing, and although we do not have a pope, we have great cardinals and bishops.

I have also been privileged through the years to know some of the brightest lights in the investment business. Their influence on me is difficult to measure, but definitely significant. Walter Schloss has hung his hat at Tweedy since 1954 and at 89 is someone who can definitely be called a legend of the investment world. Special thanks to Paul F. Miller, a founder of Miller, Anderson and Sherrard, Howard Marks, of Oaktree Capital, and Byron Wien whose commentary and anlyses of investments and investment trends have always sharpened my own thinking. And in my Hall of Fame, I have to include Marty Whitman, an octogenarian who is still running at full speed; and Jean-Marie Eveillard who retired last year after many years as a true value investor for reasons I do not understand. Value investing is the stress-free route to investment success. Maybe that is why I will think about retirement when I hit 90, although Irving Kahn just passed 100 with no slowdown in sight.

Last, thanks to Tim Melvin, a client and friend without whose writing talent, this book might never have been.

While I have worked at Tweedy, Browne Company LLC for many years, I should note that this book contains my personal and candid views on investing and does not necessarily represent the views of Tweedy, Browne Company LLC.

# Introduction

*You need to invest but you don't need to be a genius to do it smartly.*

More people own stocks today than at any time in the past. Stock markets around the world have grown as more people embrace the benefits of capitalism to increase their wealth. Yet how many people have taken the time to understand what investing is all about? My suspicion is, not very many.

Making knowledgeable investment decisions can have a significant impact on your life. It can provide for a comfortable retirement, send your children to college, and provide the financial freedom to indulge all sorts of fantasies. And sensible investing, which can be found in the art and science of the tenets of value investing, is not rocket science. It merely requires understanding a few sound principles that anyone with an average IQ can master.

Value investing has been around as an investment philosophy since the early

1930s. The principles of value investing were first articulated in 1934 when Benjamin Graham, a professor of investments at Columbia Business School, wrote a book titled *Security Analysis,* the first, and still the best, book on investing. It has been read by millions through the years. So, value investing is not the new-new. It is, in fact, the old-old. This approach to investing is easy to understand, has greater appeal to common sense, and, I believe, has produced superior investment results for more years than any competing investment strategy.

Value investing is not a set of hard-and-fast rules. It is a set of principles that form a philosophy of investing. It provides guidelines that can point you in the direction of good stocks, and just as importantly, steer you away from bad stocks. Value investing brings to the field a model by which you can evaluate an investment opportunity or an investment manager. While investment performance is measured against a benchmark like the Standard & Poor's 500 or the Morgan Stanley Capital International global and international indices, value investing provides a standard by which other investment strategies can be measured.

Why value investing? Because it has worked since anyone began tracking returns. A mountain of evidence confirms that the principles of value investing have provided market-beating returns over long periods. And it is easy to do. Value investing takes the field out of the arcane and into the realm of easy comprehension. Yet in the face of compelling evidence, few investors and few professional money managers subscribe to the principles of value investing. By some estimates, only 5 percent to 10 percent of professional money managers adhere to those principles. We'll talk about why so few investors find value investing appealing and why this matters to you later. But first, I will explain the basic principles value investors bring to bear in their research and analysis, show you how you can apply it to find opportunities around the globe, and let you decide if it is all that difficult. As Warren Buffett has said, no more than 125 IQ points are needed to be a successful investor. Any more and they are wasted.

## You Are Who You Meet

My firm, where I have toiled since 1969, was founded in 1920 by Forest Berwind Tweedy (aka Bill Tweedy). Bill Tweedy was an eccentric character who looked more like Wilfred Brimley than the dashing stockbrokers of the 1920s. When he started the firm, he looked for a business niche with little competition. He found it in stocks that were seldom traded. Typically, one shareholder or a small group of shareholders held the majority interest in the company. However, in numerous cases, there were minority shareholders who had no market for their shares other than to offer them back to the company. Bill Tweedy saw an opportunity. He would try to put together the minority buyers and sellers. He did this by seeking out shareholders at the annual meetings. He would send them a postcard asking if they wanted to buy or sell some of their shares, and so he became a specialist in closely held and inactively traded stocks.

Tweedy worked at a rolltop desk in a spare office on Wall Street in New York. He had no assistant, no secretary. And he did this for 25 years. In 1945, my father, Howard Browne, and a friend of his, Joe Reilly, left their jobs at different firms where they were not happy and went into partnership with Tweedy; and Tweedy, Browne and Reilly was born. The three wanted to continue the business of making markets in inactively traded and closely held securities that sold at below market prices.

Tweedy's activities attracted the attention of Benjamin Graham in the early 1930s and they developed a brokerage relationship. When Tweedy, Browne, and Reilly was formed in 1945, the partners took office space at 52 Wall Street down the hall from Graham. They thought that being near him would get them a larger share of Graham's business.

The firm struggled through the 1940s and the 1950s, but it survived. There were enough eccentric investors who liked cheap stocks that were not listed on exchanges to keep the firm going. In 1955, Walter Schloss, who had worked for Graham and left in 1954 to start his own investment partnership, moved into the Tweedy, Browne, and Reilly offices at a desk in a hallway next to the watercooler and the coatrack. Schloss practiced pure Graham value investing, and he racked up a 49-year record of compounding at nearly 20 percent. While he still maintains an office at my firm, he retired a few years ago when as a widower, he remarried at age 87. (Don't worry about Walter's future. Both his parents made it to 100+.)

Walter introduced two key people to the firm. In 1957, Bill Tweedy retired as did Ben Graham. My father and Joe Reilly liked having three partners. Walter introduced them to Tom Knapp who had attended Columbia Business School when Graham was teaching and had worked for him. He became the third partner because he realized that a lot of naïve people offered Tweedy, Browne cheap stocks. His idea was to change the firm into a money management business.

Walter's second introduction was another associate of the Graham firm, Warren Buffett. Financial lore says that Graham offered to turn his fund over to Buffett, but Buffett's wife wanted to move back to Omaha, Nebraska. So poor Buffett had to start over. In 1959, Walter Schloss introduced Warren Buffett to my father beginning a relationship based on trust that lasted for 10 years until Buffett closed down his partnership in 1969. My father bought most of the Berkshire Hathaway that Buffett owns today. Tweedy, Browne had the advantage of being broker to three of the most outstanding investors in history: Benjamin Graham, Walter Schloss, and Warren Buffett. No wonder we are committed value investors.

Think of the search for value stocks like grocery shopping for the highest quality goods at the best possible price. This little book will explain the underpinnings of the investment philosophy of the consistently outstanding investors so that you may learn how to stock the shelves of your value store with the highest quality, lowest cost merchandise we can find.

## Chapter One

# Buy Stocks like Steaks ... On Sale

*Buy stocks like you buy everything else, when they are on sale.*

On Sale are two of the most compelling words in advertising. Imagine that you are in the supermarket, strolling down the aisles gathering your groceries for the week ahead. In the meat aisle, you discover that one of your favorites, prime Delmonico steak, is on sale—down to just $2.50 per pound from the usual $8.99 per pound. What do you do? You load up the cart with this delicacy while it's cheaply priced. When you return the next week and see those Delmonico steaks priced at $12.99 a pound, you pause. Perhaps this week, chicken or pork might be a smarter buy. This is how most people shop. They check the sales flyers stuffed in the Sunday newspaper and make their purchases when they spot a bargain on something they want or need. They wait until they see that dishwasher or refrigerator on sale no matter how much they want or need a new one. Every holiday, they flock to the mall to take advantage of the huge bargains that are only offered a few times during the year. When interest rates drop, they run to the bank or mortgage broker to refinance or take out new and bigger mortgages. Most people tend to look at pretty much everything they buy with an eye on the value they get for the price they pay. When prices drop, they buy more of the things they want and need. Except in the stock market.

In the stock market, there is the irresistible excitement and lure of the hot stocks everyone is talking about at cocktail parties—the ones that are the darlings of the talking heads on cable stock market shows, and the financial newsletters tell us that we must own. It is the wave of the future! It is a new paradigm! People believe that they'll miss a terrific opportunity if they don't own these super exciting stocks. It is not just average Janes and Joes who get caught up in the frenzy. When stocks climb, Wall Street research reports scream *Buy.* When stocks fall, the experts tell us to *Hold* when they really mean *Sell.* (Sell is considered impolite in the world of stocks except under the most extreme circumstances.) Everyone seems to think that they should buy stocks that are rising and sell those that are falling.

There are reasons for this pattern of behavior: First, investors are afraid of being left behind and like the idea of owning the hot and popular stocks everyone is talking about. They also find a certain comfort in knowing that lots of other people have made the same choices (like fans cheering for the same sports team). But it's not just everyday, individual investors who fall prey to the herd mentality; it also happens to professional portfolio managers. If they own the same stocks everyone else owns, they are unlikely to be fired if the stocks go down. After all, they won't look quite so bad compared with their peers, who will also be down. This unique situation fosters a mind-set that allows investors to be comfortable losing money as long as everyone else is losing money, too.

The other reason investors fall prey to the fads and follow the crowd is that investors, both individual and professional, tend to become disillusioned when the stocks they own or stock markets in general decline significantly. They end up with a bad taste in their mouths that prevents them from buying stocks while the value of their retirement funds is falling. When stocks go down, people lose money. The news—on the television, in the papers—seems all doom and gloom. Investors get scared.

However, buying stocks should not be so different from buying steak on sale or waiting for the car companies to offer special incentives. In fact, the Internet has made bargain buyers of everyone: You can buy used books from stores in the United Kingdom, computers from sellers in Canada, and jeans on sale in Japan. You don't really care where the seller is—you just want the bargain (often found on eBay)—and in our increasingly borderless world, the "stores" you shop at are not limited to those that are a short drive away.

The same holds for stocks. The time to buy stocks is when they are on sale, and not when they are high priced because everyone wants to own them. I have been investing for myself and clients for more than 30 years, and I always try to buy stocks on sale, no matter where the sale is. Buying stocks when they are cheap has for me been the best way to grow my money. Stocks of good companies on sale reaped the highest returns. They have beaten both the market and the more glamorous and exciting issues being chatted about at cocktail parties or around the watercooler at work.

Hot stocks (or *growth* stocks, in financial world parlance) have always been considered the more exciting and interesting form of investing. But are they the most profitable? When people invest in growth stocks, they are hoping to invest in companies that have a product or service that is in high demand and will grow faster than the rest of the marketplace. Growth investors tend to own the darlings of the day—hot new products or companies with lots of sex appeal. They tend to be the best among their industry group and innovators in their field. There is nothing wrong with owning great businesses that can grow at fast rates. The fault in this approach lies in the price that investors pay. Nothing grows at superhigh rates forever. Eventually, hypergrowth slows. In the interim, investors have often bid the prices of these hot, glamour stocks up to unsustainable heights. When growth rates decline, the result can be injurious to the investor's financial well-being.

One of the best ways to look at which method of investing will give us the best results is to review real-world results of mutual funds. Almost everyone invests in mutual funds these days, frequently through retirement (401(k) or IRA) accounts. There are many kinds of mutual funds, but the two most popular are *growth funds,* which invest in hot new companies, and *value funds,* which buy stocks on sale. The research service Morningstar does a great job of tracking fund results and ranking them by category. The funds are divided into categories according to their investment strategy—whether they invest in large, medium-size, or small companies (large, mid, and small caps, in Wall Street jargon)—as well as whether they favor a growth or value style. What Morningstar statistics show is that no matter what size company the funds invest in, the value funds earn the best returns over the long term. This turns out to be true not just among funds investing in U.S. companies but funds that invest in companies all over the globe.

Over the past five years, value funds have outperformed growth funds by 4.87 percent annually compounded. This is remarkable when you consider that the press frequently hails professional investors who beat the markets by a penny or two. There are those who would have you believe that it is impossible to beat the market over long periods. They write off the track records of stock market legends such as Warren Buffett, Bill Ruane, or Bill Miller as lucky accidents. This is based on a theory, known as the *efficient market hypothesis,* that is taught in many college classrooms. The theory basically claims there are no "cheap" or "rich" stocks, that the market is a rational, intelligent entity that perfectly prices each stock every day based on the known information. Anyone who beats the market is just plain lucky.

Warren Buffett sees it otherwise. In a now legendary speech he made in 1984 on the fiftieth anniversary of the publication of *Security Analysis* (and later printed in *Hermes,* the Columbia Business School magazine) as "The Super Investors of Graham and Doddsville," Buffett used the example of 225 million Americans each betting one dollar on a coin flip. Each day, the losers drop out and the winners go on to the next round, with all winnings being bet the next day. After just 20 days, there will be 215 people who have won just over a million dollars. The proponents of the efficient market hypothesis would have us believe that those who outperform the market are nothing more than lucky coin flippers. Mr. Buffett furthers the analogy, swapping orangutans for people. The result is the same: 215 furry orange winners. But what if all the winning orangutans came from the same zoo? This would raise a few questions as to how these giant fur balls learned this amazing skill. Was it luck, or did all the orangutans have something in common? Buffett then looked at the world of investing and examined the record of some of the most successful investors of all time. The seven super investors were all found to be from the same zoo, so to speak. Several of the investors cited by Buffett had either taken Graham's course at Columbia Business School or worked for him at his investment firm. All were committed value types in the mold of Graham and subscribed to the basic concept of buying businesses for less than they are worth. And all had made better returns than the overall stock market and their more growth-oriented peers.

Each of these alleged lucky coin flippers did not apply value principles in exactly the same way. And they did not own the same stocks. Some owned a lot of stocks. Others owned only a few. Their portfolios were quite different. However, they all had a common intellectual grounding, and they believed in the basic concept of value investing—buying a business for far less than it is worth. This is not lucky coin flipping but buying stocks on sale.

This concept is supported by rigorous academic studies of value investing versus growth, or as some call it, "glamour investing." These studies make a compelling case that buying the cheapest stocks based on simple principles produces better results. From 1968 to 2004, value portfolio characteristics produced superior returns. In many cases, the degree of outperformance in these studies was several percentage points greater. But don't just take my word for it. In "Don't Take My Word for It" at the end of this little book, there is a quick tour through the empirical evidence. You don't have to read all these studies, but understanding the research and results will help you better appreciate the tremendous advantage that value investing provides.

A few percentage points of better performance can have a huge impact on your net worth. Suppose you invested $10,000 in your retirement account, and it compounded at 8 percent for 30 years, the average time one saves for retirement. By the time you were ready to retire, you would have just over $100,000. A tidy sum! However, if you could compound that same $10,000 over the same 30 years at 11 percent, your nest egg would grow to nearly $229,000. That would make a big difference in the way you would spend your retirement years. Just as it makes sense to buy steaks, cars, and jeans on sale, it makes sense to buy stocks on sale, too. Stocks on sale will give you more value in return for your dollars.

# Chapter Two

# What's It Worth?

*Think like a banker.*

The beauty of value investing is its logical simplicity. It is based on two principles: What's it worth (intrinsic value), and don't lose money (margin of safety). These concepts were introduced by Benjamin Graham in 1934, and they are as relevant today as they were then.

Graham began as a credit analyst. When bankers make a loan, they first look at the collateral the borrower has to pledge to secure the loan. Next, they look at the borrower's income for paying the interest on the loan. If a borrower earns $75,000 a year and wants to take out a $125,000 mortgage on a $250,000 house, that is a pretty safe bet. It is not so safe a bet if someone earning $40,000 a year wants to borrow $300,000 to buy a $325,000 house. Graham applied the same principles to analyzing stocks.

Stocks are not unlike houses. When you apply for a mortgage, the bank sends an appraiser to value the house you want to buy. In the same way, a value analyst acts like an appraiser trying to estimate the value of a business. It is in this concept that Graham's definition of intrinsic value originates. It is the price that would be paid if a company were sold by a knowledgeable owner to a knowledgeable buyer in an arm's-length negotiated transaction.

Few investors, individual or professional, pay much attention to intrinsic value, but it is important for two reasons: It enables investors to determine if a particular stock is a bargain relative to what a buyer of the entire company would pay, and it lets investors know if a stock they own is overvalued. The overvalued part of the equation is even more important if you want to avoid losing money. At year-end 1999, the price of Microsoft stock peaked at $58.89. In the seven years leading up to 1999, Microsoft's earnings per share had increased 775 percent from 8 cents per share to 70 cents per share. A terrific company with a stellar record of growth. However, was it worth 84 times earnings at the end of 1999? Apparently not. Over the next six years through 2005, Microsoft's earnings per share grew 87 percent to $1.31. While this is still an enviable growth rate, it is far less than the growth the company enjoyed in the 1990s. The result was that by the first quarter of 2006, Microsoft was trading at less than half its share price on December 31, 1999, and its price-to-earnings ratio had declined from more than 75 times earnings to approximately 20 times earnings. Investors who bought Microsoft in late 1999 own shares in a great company, but they may have to wait many years to get their money back.

Louis Lowenstein, a professor at Columbia University, scoured the universe of investors to see if there were any professional investors who survived the "perfect financial storm" of 1999 through 2003, a period that saw the NASDAQ Composite Index soar, collapse, and only partly rebound. Were there money managers who avoided the boom-and-bust cycle of this period—who did not own the technology, telecommunication, and media stocks or the Enrons or WorldComs that were the investment darlings of the day? How did they do over this period? Lowenstein found 10 value mutual funds that racked up an average 10.8 percent annually compounded rate of return over the four-year period compared with annually compounded losses for all the major U.S. stock indexes. Only one fund owned a darling of the day, and that was only for a brief period.

The hot stocks of that time would never compute under the principle of intrinsic value. By sticking to their principles, the managers of these 10 mutual funds not only saved their shareholders from huge losses, but even made money for them in a period where even an investor in an index fund lost money. The August 2000 issue of *Fortune* magazine included an article titled "10 Stocks to Last the Decade." The recommended stocks (which were described as "Here's a buy-and-forget portfolio" that would let you "retire when ready") were Broadcom, Charles

Schwab, Enron, Genentech, Morgan Stanley, Nokia, Nortel Networks, Oracle, Univision, and Viacom. Lowenstein found that by the end of 2002, these 10 stocks had suffered an average loss of 80 percent. And even after a market rebound in 2003, the aggregate loss was still 50 percent. Maybe you could retire if you don't mind eating cold beans out of a can and living in a tent.

Why is intrinsic value so important? Don't stock prices just fluctuate up and down having nothing to do with their intrinsic values? It is true that stocks will from time to time sell for more or less than intrinsic value. Some investors like to play the market by jumping on trends in stock prices. This is called momentum investing. If a stock is rising, they like to buy it hoping they will know when to get out before it falls. However, this type of investing may require a knowledge that is more divine than earthbound. Intrinsic value is important because it lets the investor take advantage of temporary mispricing of stocks. If a stock is selling for less than its intrinsic value, chances are this will ultimately be recognized and the market price will rise to a level more indicative of the company's worth. Or the company may choose to sell out at its intrinsic value, or a corporate raider may come along and try to take it over at a price that reflects something closer to intrinsic value. If a stock is priced way over intrinsic value, it may become vulnerable to the "king is wearing no clothes syndrome." This is what happened in the spring of 2000 when the technology, media, and telecommunications bubble burst. Investors realized that a lot of those new age Internet stocks never had a chance of developing into real businesses with real profits that would justify their lofty stock prices. The result was a dramatic downward revaluation of many of those "had to own" stocks.

The consequences of the stock market revaluing overpriced stocks is often what Graham and I call "permanent capital loss." If the stock price of a mundane company declines, which it often does, you have the comfort of knowing that it is still worth more than you paid for it, and someday the price is likely to recover. If a stock is grossly overvalued and its stock price crashes, history shows that it is unlikely it will regain its former inflated value. Does the investor who bought JDS Uniphase for more than $140 per share, only to see it crash to less than $2 per share, think he will ever see $140 per share again? History says no. This is permanent capital loss. And it has happened numerous times over the years. The 1990s' bubble is only the latest example. The same sequence of events happened in the early 1970s when investors bid up the price of a group of favorite growth stocks dubbed the "Nifty Fifty" to absurd levels. The losses on those stocks were in the 70 percent+range and many of them were real businesses, unlike the concept stocks of the 1990s.

How do I determine intrinsic value? There are two broad approaches to determining intrinsic value. The first is highly statistical and involves a set of financial ratios that are good indicators of value. By observing the financial characteristics of stocks that perform well, we can construct a model for a good, cheap stock. This method is not unlike the way GEICO screens for good drivers. It gathers data on drivers with good records and drivers with bad records to create a profile, or model, of what good drivers look like. If GEICO only issues auto insurance policies to drivers between the age of 35 and 55 who live in the suburbs but take public transportation to work, who have no children of driving age, and who own and drive a multi-air-bagged Volvo, the company will have to cover fewer accidents than other companies that insure teenage boys who drive sports cars. A similar model can be derived for stocks.

The other approach to determining intrinsic value, I call the appraisal method. This method involves making a company-specific estimate of what the stock would be worth if the company were sold to a knowledgeable buyer in an open auction. It is very much the same process you would follow to sell your house. You would call a few local real estate brokers whose knowledge of recent sales in your neighborhood would guide them to a suggested listing price for your house. This is what a company board of directors often does when they vote to sell their company, only they employ brokers who go by the fancy title of investment banker. The bankers look for recent acquisitions of companies in the same or a related industry to guide them in appraising a particular company.

In a perfect world, all stocks would sell for their intrinsic value. But it is not a perfect world. That is good. It creates investment opportunities. Stock prices, for many reasons, trade for more or less than intrinsic value—often far more or far less. Most investors are driven by emotions that run the gamut from extreme pessimism to jubilant optimism. These emotions can drive stock prices to the extremes of overvaluation and undervaluation. The job for the smart investor is to recognize when this is happening and to take advantage of the emotional swings of the market. Warren Buffett has used the analogy of two partners who own a widget business. Their chief competitor, a knowledgeable buyer, is always trying to buy the business for $10 per share, which would be a fair estimate of its intrinsic value. Partner A is highly emotional and his view of the business's prospects is prone to sudden change. One day, the company gets a big order from Wal-Mart, and he is ecstatic. He offers to buy out partner B for $15 per share thinking the business is about to take off. The next week, Wal-Mart trims its order as does Sears. He is depressed. He thinks he will lose everything and offers to sell his share of the business for $5 per share. This happens all the time. If partner B remains calm and detached, he can take advantage of partner A's irrational behavior and either sell at a premium or buy at a discount. Since partner B can't influence partner A's emotional swings, just as investors can't influence the emotions of the stock market, he has to sit back and wait for partner A to overreact to what he perceives as good news or bad news. This is what rational value investors do. They sit back and wait for the market to offer stocks for less than they are worth and to buy the same stocks back for more than they are worth.

## Chapter Three

# Belts and Suspenders for Stocks

*First rule of investing:*
*Don't lose money.*
*Second rule of investing:*
*Refer to rule number one.*

Benjamin Graham was a cautious investor who took a "belts and suspenders" approach to stock picking. Once he had accepted the concept of intrinsic value as a method of determining what a company was worth, he applied it to the field of investing to get an edge over the market. He had to buy stocks selling for less than intrinsic value. He was first a credit analyst: If a company was worth X, he wanted to invest in it at less than X. Like a banker, he looked for his margin of safety, his "collateral." If he was wrong, or if some unforeseen event reduced his estimate of a company's value, he wanted a cushion. He wanted belts and suspenders for his stocks. The premise was that if he bought shares in a company for less than they were worth to a knowledgeable buyer of the entire company, he had a margin of safety. These are sound lending principles and should be sound investing principles.

Think about it—before Graham, the world of investing was composed mostly of speculators and stock manipulators. But anyone who had followed his principles would have avoided most of the financial carnage of the crash of 1929 just as true value investors avoided the bursting of the technology bubble in 2000. As Warren Buffett has advised, the first rule of investing is, don't lose money. The second rule is, don't forget rule number one.

Most companies increase their net worth, or intrinsic value, over time. If intrinsic value is your benchmark, you can profit in two ways. First, the value of the shares you own will increase while you own them. Second, if the price of the stock rises from less than intrinsic value to intrinsic value over time, you will have a win/win situation. When you pay full price for a stock—a price equal to its intrinsic value—your future gains may be limited to the company's internal rate of growth and any dividends it may pay you. If you think of the Standard & Poor's 500 stock index as a giant conglomerate with 500 divisions, you will observe that over long periods, its earnings have grown on average about 6 percent per year. Typically, 3 percent of the increase has come from the growth of Gross National Product, and 3 percent has come from inflation. Therefore, the intrinsic value of the S&P 500 thought of as a single company increases about 6 percent a year. In addition, the S&P 500 pays a dividend. Historically, the dividend yield of the S&P 500 has been in the range of 3 percent to 4 percent. Take the sum of the long-term earnings growth (6 percent) and the dividend yield (4 percent), and you get a long-term annually compounded rate of return for the S&P 500 of about 10 percent. This is the return investors in an index fund expect to make over the long term. And if they stay in the index fund long enough, they should get that return.

Investing in stocks is not like putting your money in a savings account that pays 10 percent annually. Returns will fluctuate from year to year, sometimes dramatically. The 10 percent return is only an average of some bang-up years, and some gut-wrenching years. What you would like is some mechanism that forces you into the market when stocks are cheap and eases you out when they are dear. Getting in at the bottom of a stock market cycle produces better returns than getting in at the top.

While Graham did not make pronouncements about the level of the broader stock market, he had a formula for identifying whether individual stocks were cheap or expensive. He used this formula to guide his individual stock selections.

Basically, Graham wanted to buy stocks selling at two-thirds or less of their intrinsic value. This was his margin of safety, the belt for his stocks. It is a margin of safety for a couple of reasons. First, if he was correct in his estimate of intrinsic value, the stock could rise 50 percent and still not be overvalued. Second, if the stock market hit a rough patch, he had the comfort of knowing that what he owned was ultimately worth more than he paid for it.

A margin of safety gives you an edge over just blindly buying stocks or an index fund. Over the years, our margin of safety in the stocks we buy has provided more of our overall gain than the underlying growth in the value of the business. If we buy the stock of ABC Ice Cream Corporation for $6.50 and we believe it is worth $10.00, we have a potential gain of $3.50. If during the period we own the stock, the company can grow its business by 10 percent so that the stock becomes worth $11.00, we have a larger potential gain. However, the greatest part of that gain has come from buying the stock cheaply in the first place. If an investor had bought the same stock for $10.00, his potential gain might only be $1.00. Buying dollars for 66 cents has produced market-beating returns for many value investors.

Buying stocks at a discount to their intrinsic value not only is the belt for stocks, but also serves as a set of suspenders for what it prevents investors from doing. We have generally avoided investing in companies that have a lot of debt relative to their net worth. This margin of safety provides assurance that the company will survive during poor economic times such as a recession. We all know people who seek the maximum mortgage on their house, run up their credit card debts to the limit, and live from paycheck to paycheck. We also know people who maintain a rainy-day fund to get them through unforeseen rough patches. If the guy with all the debt loses his job, he may lose his house as well. The guy with the rainy-day fund can survive until he gets another job. The same is true for companies. A company with a lot of debt where earnings barely cover the interest expense is a far riskier investment than a company with some extra cash on its balance sheet. It is all about having a cushion—a margin of safety—to get you through the bad times that people and companies inevitably encounter.

The other downside of high debt is that companies or individuals cede a measure of control over their affairs to a lender. When times are good, it is easy to borrow money. When times are bad and you really need the money you have borrowed, that is usually the time the banker calls looking to be repaid. Whether it is a company running up debt to pay for expenses, or a person borrowing to buy stocks on margin, the borrower is giving someone else the right to say when the game is over.

Another principle of margin of safety is diversification. Like Graham, I want to have a broadly diversified portfolio both in terms of the number of stocks we own, and in terms of spreading those investments over different industries. Individual stocks and particular industries can have the wind in their face from time to time. Such adverse conditions are difficult to predict. They just happen. We call them *negative event surprises.* Accidents happen and no amount of advance planning can insulate you completely from such occurrences. If it were possible, every year on January 1, we would pick the two stocks we thought would be the best performers for the coming year. If we could do this successfully and consistently, our investment results would be off the charts. We would just have to be willing to bet the ranch.

But some things are easier said than done. In any given year, every stock portfolio will hold winners and losers, and it's virtually impossible to sidestep every loser. The point is to hold more winners than losers. The concept is a bit like being in the insurance business. Insurance companies try very hard to identify potential risks, but also realize they can never be 100 percent correct. If an insurance company only issued one policy a year and that policyholder did not have a claim, the company would make out like gangbusters. However, if that one policy holder had an accident, the insurance company would be in deep trouble. This is why insurance companies issue lots of policies. They want to get the average accident rate that their selection criteria can produce, and they do not want to drown in a sea of accident claims. The same goal holds true for stocks. You try to avoid investing in stocks that have a greater likelihood of losing value, but there are times when something may go wrong. By diversifying, you provide yourself with insurance that if one of your stocks blows up, it will not severely impact your net worth.

How much diversification should one have? The answer to that question depends on your tolerance for risk. Certainly, 10 stocks in a portfolio is a minimum. Other investors like to own as many as 50 or even 100 if they can find that many meeting their criteria. You should ask yourself: If one of my stocks went bankrupt could I just slough it off?

The last and perhaps greatest benefit of margin of safety investing is that it allows you to be a contrarian. Investing counter to the herd is not easy. We are all influenced by what we read in newspapers, see on TV, or hear from friends or people we consider experts. The best time to buy stocks is when they are cheap. However, when stocks are at their cheapest, there are usually a whole host of reasons not to buy them. I recall 1973 and 1974 when the Nifty Fifty growth stocks of the late 1960s and early 1970s crashed bringing the broader market indices down about 50 percent, and the United States underwent a major oil price shock. Maybe value investors were simpletons to go on a buying spree, but we all felt like kids in a candy store. The same was true in 1981 when four years of economic mismanagement by the Carter presidency drove U.S. interest rates through the roof. Only a fool would buy stocks. But the years following 1974 and 1981 were some of the best years to be invested.

Following the principles of value investing, if stocks are cheap, you buy them. You forget all the noise that is swirling around you and take advantage of stocks on sale. The reverse is also true. If stocks are dear, if valuations are reaching or exceeding intrinsic value and there is no margin of safety, you sell. More than likely, you will be selling when every one else is buying. Not to worry. That is what a successful investor is supposed to do. These two simple investment principles, intrinsic value and margin of safety, provide the courage and the reassurance that buying in bad times and selling in good times is the better course to follow.

# Chapter Four

# Buy Earning son the Cheap

*The lower the price, the higher the return.*

A tried-and-true method of successful investing is to buy stocks selling at a low multiple of their earnings. Earnings are what a company has left after it has paid all its bills. Ben Graham once remarked that earnings are the principal factor driving stock prices. If I accept this as truth, and I do, then the less I pay for a stock when compared with earnings, the better my future return should be. Makes sense, right? I primarily measure earnings-to-stock price by comparing the price-to-earnings (P/E) ratio, to other companies and the broader stock market indices.

The P/E ratio is easily determined. It is the company's stock price divided by its profit, usually reported as earnings per share. If the ABC Ice Cream Corporation earned $1 million last year and had 1 million shares outstanding, the earnings per share (or EPS as it is often called) would be $1. If the stock price was $10, the P/E ratio would be 10. If the price of the stock was $20, then the ratio would be 20. Some investors refer to the inverse of this as the *earnings yield.* It reflects the return you would receive if all the earnings were paid out in cash as a dividend rather then reinvested in the company. The earnings yield is calculated by dividing the earnings per share by the stock price. A stock with a P/E of 20 has an earnings yield of 5 percent; a highflier with an earnings multiple of 40 would have an earnings yield of 2.5 percent. Remember: The lower the PE, the higher the earnings yield.

The concept of earnings yield is helpful when comparing investment opportunities. Graham did this. For example, a stock selling at 10 times earnings has an earnings yield of 10 percent. Compare this with a 10-year Treasury note yielding 5 percent, and you get twice the return. If you bought a 10-year Treasury note today for $1,000, it would pay you $50 per year and return your $1,000 when it matures in 10 years. Nothing is safer in terms of absolute dollars. But there is a catch. Let's say over the next 10 years, inflation is 3 percent per year, which is close to its historic average. (Inflation was much higher in the 1970s and the 1980s, and is a bit lower than 3 percent in the first half of the current decade.) The $1,000 the U.S. Treasury returns to you in 10 years is only worth $737 in today's money. Even with fairly modest inflation rates, the value of the purchasing power of your Treasury note investment has declined by 26.3 percent.

If you buy a stock at 10 times earnings (a 10 percent earnings yield), you are getting twice the return if the company theoretically paid out all the earnings. Few companies do. Instead, they give you a portion of the earnings in the form of a dividend, and reinvest the balance in the business to finance their growth. Corporations also have the advantage that they can often pass the cost of inflation on to their customers. With no growth in the amount of ice cream they sell, ABC Ice Cream Corporation can probably raise the price of its ice cream by at least the rate of inflation. If the $1 of earnings you bought for $10 grows at the rate of inflation, it will be $1.34 at the end of 10 years. At the same P/E ratio, the stock would be worth $13.40. Generally, corporate earnings grow at the rate of inflation and the rate of growth of the economy, historically 3 percent. Added together, inflation plus overall economic growth would mean that your original $1 of earnings would grow at 6 percent per annum. The earnings per share would then be $1.79 in 10 years; $1,000 invested in the stock at the same P/E ratio, 10 years later would be worth $1,739.

Why is this important to your financial health? Because if inflation is 3 percent, $1,000 invested today has to be worth $1,344 in 10 years just to maintain your purchasing power. The Treasury note can't do that. Stocks can.

Whether we think about our return in terms of P/E ratios or earnings yields, it is all the same. Wall Street analysts tend to look at P/E ratios from two perspectives. There is the *trailing* P/E ratio, which is the stock price divided by the most recent fiscal year or past four quarters of earnings. Then there is the *forward* P/E ratio, which is the stock price divided by analysts' estimates of how much a company will earn in the next year or next four quarters. Most stocks trade based on what the market thinks the company will earn in the future. The past is the past. Warren Buffett says that basing investment decisions on trailing earnings is investing by looking through the rearview mirror.

When it comes to projecting earnings, however, the track record of Wall Street analysts is spotty at best and highly inaccurate at worst. When noted investor David Dreman looked at analyst estimates from 1973 to 1993, a period containing 78,695 separate quarterly estimates, he found that there was only a 1 in 170 chance that the analyst projections would fall within plus or minus 5 percent of the actual number. Corporate earnings are full of surprises; some positive, some negative.

Were it possible to truly know the future, you could make a bundle. Graham's focus was to look for companies with a reasonably stable record of earnings, a degree of predictability, rather than to search vainly for the specific future earnings estimates that Wall Street seeks. With that in mind, it is still better to just buy the cheapest stocks based on earnings that have already been tallied, audited, and reported to the shareholders.

Over the years, numerous studies have examined the results of buying stocks at low P/E ratios versus buying high price/earnings ratio stocks (the high-growth companies and market darlings). Each study—over time periods from 1957 to virtually the present, and measured over a period of 5 years to nearly 20 years—confirms that buying cheaper, less popular stocks brings far greater returns. This holds true across industries and developed countries. But don't just take my word for it. Take a look at the study results described in "Don't Take My Word for It." It will give you the courage to stay the course when the wind seems to be blowing harshly in your face. Value investing, buying earnings cheaply, is the most reliable way I know to grow your nest egg, not because I say so, but because it's also been shown to be so—time and again, throughout the decades in numerous academic studies.

The earnings, as reported by most major companies, are a starting point, but just a starting point. These numbers can frequently be misleading and may contain large one-time charges and credits that mask the true earnings of the company. Some finance professionals prefer to use cash flow, or operating earnings. Cash flow is the reported earnings with all noncash expenses such as depreciation and amortization added back. Free cash flow is cash flow minus the capital expenditures that are needed to maintain the assets of the company. Put another way, if I owned the business, how much money could I take out each year and still keep the doors open?

I also look at low price-to-earnings opportunities in terms of what they might be worth to a potential acquirer, particularly a leveraged buyout, or LBO, firm. When companies make acquisitions of other companies, they not only look at free cash flow, they look at earnings before interest expense and income taxes. This is the best measure of how much money a company is earning. Interest expense is merely a function of how much debt a company has. An acquirer could choose to keep the debt or pay it off. The acquirer is most interested in knowing how much cash a business is producing. Professionals call this cash *earnings before interest, taxes, depreciation, and amortization* (EBITDA). It is sort of a top line earnings number that shows how much cash would be available to an owner of the entire business to use for paying interest or reinvesting in the business. When companies are bought by leveraged buyout firms, the LBO firm typically uses a lot of debt to finance the purchase. EBITDA is a way of measuring the cash that would be available to service that debt.

The low price relative to earnings approach has led to some of the best investment opportunities I have seen in my career. In 1999, you could buy shares in Republic New York bank at $39 based on this type of analysis; it was bought out by HSBC in three months for $72. Stocks that sold at single-digit multiples of earnings through the years include such household names as Chase Manhattan and Wells Fargo. Taking a businesslike approach to evaluating businesses when they sell at a low price-to-earnings ratio and viewing them through the lens of a rational buyer allowed valued investors to buy shares in American Express after the travel industry decline post 9/11, and Johnson & Johnson when the health care stocks were depressed because everyone thought Hillary Clinton was going to nationalize the health care industry in 1993.

Buying low P/E stocks works in both good markets and bad markets. You just may have to wait a little longer for your return in a bear market. But the best part of following a low P/E strategy is that it forces you to buy stocks when they are cheap while fear of stocks is running high. The early 1970s was a time of bursting bubbles and soaring oil prices. The early 1980s brought pain with the colossal economic mismanagement of the Carter years and the highest inflation rates in my lifetime; Federal Reserve Bank Chairman Paul Volcker had to drive interest rates into the double digits to kill inflation. Corporate CEOs were terrified their companies would be driven out of business. During these times, all the babies got thrown out with the bathwater. But these times also provided some of the best buying opportunities in history. Such opportunities do not come on the heels of great times; they are preceded by much pain.

When stock markets are cheap in general, we are in periods of economic uncertainty. Investors have low expectations for returns going forward. Recessions, high interest rates, war threats, and other malaise rule the day. Fortunately, periods like this are the exception. Mostly, the world gets by. Economies grow at more historic rates, and there is an ebb and flow of the fortunes of individual businesses. But just as markets can go to extremes, the valuations of individual stocks also can go to extremes. Many times throughout the cycle, companies are undervalued and overvalued. Low P/E stocks are usually low expectation companies. The stock market does not perceive them to have a bright future, perhaps because they got beat up during a down period, perhaps because they have simply fallen out of favor or there are shinier-looking stocks in the store. High P/E stocks, on the other hand, are usually high expectation stocks. Everything is going right, and investors are convinced their run of great returns will continue for many years. As the legendary manager of the Vanguard Windsor Fund, John Neff, once said to me, "Every trend goes on forever until it ends." Things change and trends do not go on forever.

The world of investing, not unlike life in general, is filled with positive and negative surprises. It is important to understand how these surprise events affect stock prices. Study after study has shown that when a low P/E, low expectation stock reports disappointing news, the effect is usually minimal. The market anticipated bad news, and there was no need to knock the price down much further. Conversely, when a low expectation stock surprises the market with good news, the price can pop. The reverse is proven to happen with high expectation stocks. If they report a good quarter, the stock does not necessarily jump. It was already priced to anticipate good news. But bad news can crater a high-expectation stock. You don't have to look any further back than the tech bubble of the 1990s to appreciate the point (and the pain). In 2000, 2001, and 2002, I compiled lists of stocks that had declined more than 90 percent. They were long lists.

Chapter Five

# Buy a Buck for 66 Cents

*Dial for dollars at one-third off.*

Just as some stocks are knocked down in price to sell low relative to their earnings, at times some shares actually sell below their net worth. This could be an overreaction to a poor earnings report or industry conditions, but when this happens, these shares become candidates for the shelves of our value investing store. Net worth is simply everything a company owns—real estate, buildings, equipment inventory, and cash, minus what it owes. Subtract what it owes from what it owns, and you get what is called *book value.* The book value per share then is simply the net worth divided by the number of shares outstanding. When searching for stocks that are a bargain compared with their asset value, we start with those companies selling below book value per share. This was one of Graham's chief investment criteria and has helped me uncover some tremendous bargains over the years. Stocks selling below book value were the original specialty of Tweedy, Browne. Bill Tweedy made markets in shares of obscure stocks that frequently sold at deep discounts to their net worth. This led to his relationship with Ben Graham, as these were exactly the type of stocks Graham was looking to purchase. Eventually it was Tom Knapp, a partner who joined the firm in 1958, who led us from brokerage to investment management by pointing out that it made a lot more sense to hang onto these undervalued shares instead of just trading them.

My first job in the business was to look through the Standard & Poor's and Moody's manuals for stocks selling below their book value. Buying stocks below book value can lead to some of the best investments you can make. For example, in 1994, National Western Life Insurance, a Texas-based life insurance and bond brokerage firm was selling for a little under half of its asset value. Since then the shares have appreciated over 600 percent. In the early 1990s, you could buy shares in the brokerage firm Jeffries and Company well below book value. Jeffries is still a public company. Its book value has compounded handsomely, and it now sells at a premium to book value. As an added bonus, Jeffries started an electronic trading firm called Investment Technology Group that was spun out to shareholders. It is now a leader in its field and trades at a significant premium to many brokerage firms. Even today, as many investors claim that book value no longer matters, about one-third of the stocks I own were purchased because they sold very cheaply compared with their book value.

I have done extensive research into the profit potential of stocks selling below book value. In the early 1980s, I examined stocks in the period from 1970 to 1981. I analyzed all 7,000 companies that were in the Compustat database during that period. I looked for companies that had at least $1 million in market capitalization and sold at no more than 140 percent of their book value. I sorted them into groups based on price-to-book value and computed their six-month, and one-, two-, and three-year performance. I found that all these groupings beat the overall market over the one-, two-, or three-year periods although in many instances they lagged for the first six months. Buying the lowest grouping, stocks selling for less than 30 percent of book value, would have turned $1 million into more than $23 million over the time frame, compared with $1 million growing to just $2.6 million in the overall market.

Just as with stocks bought cheaply compared with earnings, I do not expect you to merely take my word that stocks selling below book value have the potential for large returns. There is plenty of evidence from the scholars and researchers who study what works in the stock market (see "Don't Take My Word for It"). In fact, many of the same people who studied the effect of buying stocks at low earnings multiples also researched those selling below book value. Their results were similar: Stocks selling at low multiples to book value compared with the glamorous names performed significantly better by anywhere from 6.3 percent annually to 14.3 percent a year over periods from 1967 to the present, in the United States and outside the United States. From the esteemed Barton Biggs to Nobel Prize winners, study after study confirms that value stocks outperformed growth in every country studied (mostly the United States, the United Kingdom, and European countries) by a substantial margin.

Opening ourselves up to international investing has created more opportunities to buy stocks below book value than ever before. At a time when U.S. stocks frequently sell at a premium to book value, there are hidden gems like Dae Han Flour Mills in Korea. The mill company sold at less than one-third of book value in early 2005. It has since doubled in price. In Switzerland in 2003, I uncovered Conzetta Holding, a conglomerate with divisions in sporting goods, sheet metal, glass, real estate, and several other businesses. The company was selling at roughly one-half of book value. It appeared that the real estate was undervalued on the books and they had a lot of cash in the bank. Not only was it cheap, there also appeared to be a wide margin of safety. Over the past two years, the stock has more than doubled. Also in 2003, Volkswagen, the German auto manufacturer, sold at one-half of book value. Despite industry woes in the United States, VW has been a strong performer elsewhere and doubled in value since then. By being global in your approach to loading up your value investing store, you can find many more stocks below book value than if you confine yourself to just the United States (or any other single part of the world).

I have even found companies selling below their net cash balances. This was a favorite technique of Graham, but such situations have become less available in the U.S. market. In Japan in the 1990s, you could find broadcasting companies, homebuilders, textile firms, and even a company that sells women's lingerie via party sales à la Tupperware for less than the cash on the balance sheets. I am sure bargains like these will someday exist again in the United States, but until then, having a global focus allows me to find and invest in them today.

It doesn't seem to matter what time frame you examine or even what country you choose to explore. Buying stocks that sell cheaply when compared with their asset value works. Searching for these opportunities at home and abroad is yet another way to find candidates for your store of values.

# Chapter Six

# Around the Worldwith 80 Stocks

*There is a global search for value.*

Why invest globally? Aren't there plenty of opportunities in your own backyard? Perhaps. However, if you think of the universe of stocks as a grocery store as I do, why limit yourself to half the merchandise that exists in the world? While the United States contains approximately half the publicly traded companies in the world (out of a total pool of more than 20,000 stocks), if you expand your horizons to all the developed countries of the world, you can double your chances of finding cheap stocks. And these are not obscure risky little companies. When the top 20 corporations in the world are ranked by sales, 12 of them are headquartered in Europe and Asia. When measured by sales volume, the world's largest oil company is based in the United

Kingdom, and three of the five largest auto manufacturers are found in Germany and Japan:

| Company | Sales ($ billions) | Country |
|---|---|---|
| Wal-Mart | 285 | United States |
| BP | 285 | United Kingdom |
| Royal Dutch/Shell | 265 | Netherlands |
| Exxon Mobile | 263 | United States |
| General Motors | 193 | United States |
| Daimler Chrysler | 192 | Germany |
| Ford Motor | 170 | United States |
| Toyota Motor | 165 | Japan |
| General Electric | 152 | United States |
| Chevron | 142 | United States |
| Total | 131 | France |
| Volkswagon | 120 | Germany |
| ConocoPhillips | 118 | United States |
| Allianz | 112 | Germany |
| Citigroup | 108 | United States |
| Nippon Tel | 106 | Japan |
| AXA | 97 | France |
| IBM | 96 | United States |
| AIG | 95 | United States |
| Semins Group | 93 | Germany |

Source: Forbes, Global 2000 Special Report, March 31, 2005.

Think of the companies that produce some of the products and services you run across every day: Nestlé, ING financial services, Honda, Toyota, Glaxo Smith Kline, Bayer, Sony, Samsung, Hyundai, Mitsubishi, Carnival Cruise Lines, Fuji Film, and Heineken Beer. All are large, well-known companies whose products we use or see nearly every day of our lives. To ignore global opportunities means not investing in many of the world's largest and finest corporations.

Much of the current financial literature and the advice of high-priced consultants focuses on investing in foreign stocks to achieve global diversification. The idea seems to be that by investing outside our home base, we can protect ourselves when stock prices fall at home. With a much more global economy, however, most foreign markets tend to move in the same direction. A hiccup in New York impacts London, and today's Tokyo news is required reading in Paris. The drastic sell-offs of the early 1970s, the stock market crash of 1987, and the bubble burst in 2000 were shared across the globe so diversification offered scant protection. Likewise, the rally off the lows of 2003 seems to have spread across the globe as well. The real reason to invest with a global focus is to double the number of potential value opportunities from which we can choose.

My initial exposure to expanding the principles of value investing globally came from friends and clients around the world whom I have met over the years. It was in discussions with these contacts that I became aware of some of the extreme value opportunities around the globe.

My first foray into international stocks came in the early 1980s. A former associate of Graham's who was retired and living in Barbados told my longtime partner John Spears to look at the Japanese property and casualty insurance companies because they were selling for one-third of book value. Japan was on the rise in those days, and there were few cheap stocks listed on the Tokyo Stock Exchange. Finding Japanese insurance companies selling at one-third of book value was the value investor equivalent of waving a steak bone in front of Fido. But when John took a look, it appeared that the companies were all selling at stated book value. So John went back to Graham's associate and told him what he had found. Ben's friend told John the difference was that the Japanese insurance companies reported book value with their large investment portfolios carried at cost. With the huge run-up in stock prices in Japan, the value of the portfolios had tripled. This information was not widely known, but was filed with the Tokyo stock exchange (in Japanese, of course). So we found someone fluent in Japanese to research the insurers. Sure enough, with the security portfolios valued at market, the companies were selling at one-third of book value. We bought about eight insurance company stocks. Six months later, the regulators changed the reporting requirements to show the security portfolios at market. Once the market saw this, the stocks went up to their adjusted market value. Luck doesn't hurt in the investment world!

My next foray into international markets occurred in the mid-1980s. In my travels, I noticed that European businesspeople were not all that different from those I knew in the United States. They got up each day and went to work looking to make a profit. I also noticed that Europe was not as oriented toward the stock market as investors in the United States, and this seemed to create bargain opportunities. Instead of being put off because they were not U.S. companies, I became intrigued. The comparison with U.S. companies highlighted how cheap some of the European stocks actually were. At about the time that U.S. consumer products companies like Carnation and General Foods were being acquired at 6 to 10 times pretax earnings, we found companies like Distillers Corporation in the United Kingdom selling at 4.5 times after-tax earnings. The only negative for the company was that it happened to be incorporated in the United Kingdom, which was in an economic morass in the early days of Margaret Thatcher's prime ministership. Distillers was ultimately acquired less than a year later at a price twice its market price of 12 months earlier. We found many other mundane companies such as tobacco companies, insurance companies, insurance brokers, and banks, all at very cheap prices that represented quality value opportunities.

Naturally, my interest in taking a more global approach to investing was piqued. At that time it was not possible to take as disciplined an approach to European and Asian investing as I would normally prefer. In the United States, my partners and I had access to a database of all public companies and their SEC (Securities and Exchange Commission) filings with fairly comprehensive financial information that allowed us to quickly and easily uncover a diversified range of value opportunities. Outside the United States, no such database existed. At the time, we had a client who worked as an investment banker in London. He seemed to feel that no one was doing bottom up, stock-by-stock value investing in Europe. He kept asking us why we couldn't apply the same value criteria outside the United States. Everyone else was pretty much doing the same thing, a top-down macroeconomic type of investing with little attention paid to what a particular company was worth. Our answer was always the same: We had no database that would allow us to quickly screen and sort opportunities from among 11,000 non-U.S. stocks. This situation began to change in the early 1990s. Databases began to appear covering different countries and regions. By piecing together these various databases, we could finally screen a sufficient number of companies to come up with a diversified list of candidates. The databases varied widely as to quality and depth but by piecing together the various systems, we established a method of screening non-U.S. stocks that we could then research and analyze. I called my old friend the banker, and he became our first international portfolio client.

Although global stock markets seem to move in tandem, there are exceptions, usually resulting from some regional economic problems. In 1998 when the Internet bubble began to inflate in the United States, Japanese and European stocks were much cheaper. The cheapest U.S. stocks sold at one times book value and eight times earnings. The cheapest European stocks sold at 80 percent of book value and six times earnings, while the cheapest Japanese companies were available at just one-half their asset value. With the collapse of Asian markets in 1998, there were a lot of bargain stocks in developed Asian countries, whereas there were relatively few in the United States. The reunification of Germany in the late 1980s was another example of a time when foreign stocks were much cheaper than their U.S. counterparts. The German treasury had to print a lot of West German marks to trade for relatively worthless East German marks. This caused interest rates to rise in Germany and across the rest of Western Europe. As rising interest rates are the stock market's worst enemy, this created sell-offs in the European markets and value opportunities far in excess of what existed at the time in the U.S. markets.

In a world where many of us drive a Toyota or a Lexus, enjoy a cold Heineken or Corona with our sushi, or stop for a nice Johnny Walker and soda or Beefeater martini at happy hour; use Flonase for our allergies; have insurance or other financial products from AXA or Allianz; watch movies on a DVD player from Sony or Toshiba; and load Fuji film into our Canon Camera, it seems foolish to limit our investments to just one country. By using a global approach, you can double the potential opportunities to stock the shelves of your value investing store and also put yourself in a position to benefit when other markets and companies are cheaper than your home-based counterparts.

## Chapter Seven

# You Don't Need to Go Trekking with Dr. Livingston

*There is value in some pretty friendly countries.*

Once my partners and I decided to invest globally, we had to give some thought to where in the world we were willing to invest our money. For many people, the words *global investing* conjures up images of Dr Livingston hacking through the jungles of Africa; Juan Valdez hauling coffee down from the mountains of Colombia on his trusty burro; or perhaps even the Russian Mob, their briefcases full of cash, while driving away in flashy cars with diamond-clad women. I confess to having the same fears.

Most people are predisposed to be somewhat provincial, Americans perhaps more so. The U.S. stock markets were big enough to accommodate our investing appetites, so Americans have traditionally not ventured abroad. We also have the Securities and Exchange Commission that regulates away many of the abuses of stock market manipulators though not all. The U.S. accounting standards also create a level playing field for research and analysis. (This may be less true today than when I started in this business, but that is a topic for another day.) Americans were skeptical of foreign accounting standards and complained that European and Japanese accounting rules were not sufficiently transparent; that is, we couldn't figure them out. However, I took a different view. I figured if Hans, a portfolio manager in Zurich, could learn U.S. Generally Accepted Accounting Principles (GAAP) I should be able to learn Swiss accounting protocols. Fortunately, understanding annual reports for companies around the world has gotten a lot easier today as most companies use standardized international accounting principles.

When I started plowing through foreign annual reports, I found that

European and Japanese accounting was not a minefield of deception—it was a treasure hunt. Many European companies, for a variety of reasons, were hiding assets and understating reported earnings. They did not like paying more taxes than they had to, and they did not want to raise shareholders' expectations. One early example from 1990 was Roche Holdings, the big Swiss pharmaceutical company. A basic principle of accounting is that if you take a company's net worth or book value at the beginning of the year and add to that the earnings for the ensuing year, and subtract what it paid out to shareholders in dividends, you should end up with the year-end's net worth or book value. Not with Roche. In some years, book value increased more than the reported earnings after subtracting the dividend payments. As I dug deeper, I found that Roche had a habit of taking reserves for contingent liabilities, which had the result of reducing reported earnings. Why? Who knows? It just wanted to be conservative, especially in a particularly profitable year. Setting up reserves for potential liabilities is perfectly legitimate. Suppose the company gets sued for a faulty product or has entered into a money-losing contract, it can set up a reserve for the potential loss and deduct the loss from its earnings even if it has not yet had to pay. Banks do it all the time. They make loans hoping to get paid back, but know that a certain percentage of borrowers will default. So they set up a loan loss reserve as a percentage of total loans.

In the case of Roche, the reserves were fairly questionable. As a fictional example, it might set up a reserve along the lines of SF 150 million for the possibility of an earthquake destroying a factory in Zug, which has never had an earthquake. Since the chance of an earthquake in Zug was so remote, the Swiss tax authorities would not let them take the reserve against pretax earnings. So, poof, SF 150 million disappeared from their after tax earnings report. A few years later, Roche would reverse this questionable reserve. When an American company does this, the release of the reserve gets added back to earnings as it should. Not in Switzerland. Roche would merely add the reversed reserve to book value, net worth, without ever letting it show up as reported income. See what I mean by a treasure hunt?

Another example from about the same time was Lindt and Sprungli (L&S), a Swiss candy company. Lindt makes expensive chocolates and has a great brand name. It was and is highly profitable. When we ran across Lindt and Sprungli, it was selling for 10 times reported earnings. That was pretty cheap especially since U.S. companies had recently bought another Swiss candy company and one in Norway for more than 20 times earnings. L&S was cheap for two reasons. The Swiss stock market was down because inflation had risen to an unheard of rate of 3.5 percent. The Swiss are buggo on inflation, which may help explain why they have one of the strongest currencies in the world. And Herr Sprungli had recently divorced his wife and remarried a Scientologist follower of L. Ron Hubbard. This had spooked the Swiss stock market for fear that the new Frau Sprungli might be appointed to the board of the company. A Swiss banker friend of ours told us that the former Frau Sprungli and her children had more stock in the company than her former husband, and she had told him that if he put his new wife on the board of directors, she would fire him. The Swiss are very pragmatic.

As we pursued our due diligence of the company, we saw that in addition to selling at 10 times earnings, L&S was selling at only 3.5 times cash flow. Cash flow is pretax, pre-interest expense earnings plus noncash charges for depreciation of fixed assets like factories and machinery. This is the money a company throws off before the tax man takes his share. Something did not compute. This was too cheap. Companies are allowed to depreciate their investments in fixed assets like factories and machinery on the theory that they wear out and the company will have to build new factories and buy new machinery over time. The number of years you can use to depreciate factories and machinery is usually dictated by government tax authorities. Switzerland is different. The companies choose their depreciation schedule. By dividing the depreciation of L&S into its fixed assets, the value of its factories and machinery, it looked like its depreciation schedule was about 26 months. Now, Switzerland is not Burma. The factories are not built of bamboo. More likely, a Swiss factory could withstand anything short of a direct nuclear hit. When we asked about this, we were told that Herr Sprungli was a very conservative man. When we made an adjustment to the rate of depreciation, L&S was selling for only 7.5 times earnings. When similar companies were bought for 20 times earnings or more, L&S looked pretty cheap.

In my pursuit of global investment opportunities, I choose to invest principally in the developed countries of the world like Switzerland. I look for stable economies, as well as a reasonable form of government. The so-called emerging markets have a tendency to never quite emerge and remain unsafe and unstable places for investment. Although they can be the source of enormous speculative profits from time to time, they can also be the source of staggering, rapid losses. Look at Venezuela or Argentina. Investing in countries like this ignores the concept of having a margin of safety, and is a game I do not care to play.

For every emerging market success story, there has been a disaster of at least equal or greater proportions in these undeveloped markets. I have seen tremendous economic upheaval in places such as Russia after the collapse of the Soviet Union. The Russian markets had been a gold mine initially, and then hyperinflation hit. All the "smart guys" were buying Russian short-term notes with yields in excess of 50 percent. Seems too good to be true? It was. Russia eventually defaulted on the notes and left investors with nothing but memories of their money. By the time Russian debt was unfrozen after a 90-day trading and interest halt, the ensuing currency collapse had left Western speculators with devastating losses.

In the early 1990s, Mexico was the darling of the investing world. The Mexican market kept climbing to new highs. It appeared that Mexico had finally gained an understanding of capitalism and with its enormous store of natural resources was ready to take its rightful place among the strong economies of the world. The media proclaimed loudly that, at last, Mexico would be a first world nation. Then, a few political assassinations and a sudden currency devaluation later, we discovered that global money managers financed the entire run-up. The Mexican stock market imploded with disastrous results. Had Bill Clinton and the United States not stepped in with a generous stabilization aid package, the entire nation of Mexico might well have gone bankrupt. Needless to say, investors suffered enormous losses.

In the mid-1960s, My brother Will served in the Peace Corps in South America, where he got a lesson in Latin rule of law: Sometimes the laws work and sometimes they don't. Argentina has gone from bust to being the darling of Latin America in the 1990s. Now it is bust again. And look at the most recent disasters in Venezuela and Bolivia. Elections have brought socialist leaders who are cozying up to Fidel Castro and nationalizing foreign company assets. Why bother to invest in countries that are this unstable?

Until the late 1990s, East Asia was the darling of the emerging markets investing world. Countries such as Malaysia, Singapore, and Thailand had experienced enormous economic growth with internal growth rates as high as 8 to 12 percent. It was hailed wide and far as the Asian economic miracle. As it became evident that foreign investment, and not increased productivity, had financed all this growth, the balloon began to deflate. In 1997, with the taste of the Mexican crisis still in their mouths, investors began to flee the East Asian countries with disastrous results. In Thailand, the stock market fell over 75 percent. The Philippine market lost over one-third. In three days in October, the Hong Kong markets lost 23 percent and the government eventually spent billions to prop up local equity and currency markets. In Malaysia, the exchange lost over 50 percent. Singapore, considered one of the most stable of the East Asian tigers, dropped over 60 percent. These are not the risks that I consider to be consistent with a margin of safety.

There seems to be a boom-bust cycle in all the less developed markets. Early investors reap fast profits and then an excess flood of foreign investment and cash pushes the local economy to the point of a speculative bubble. It is a dangerous way to invest, as those left holding the bag will find the bag is empty.

As I write this, there is enormous investor interest in China. The world's most populous nation seems to be waking up to the joys of capitalism. It is growing at a very rapid pace and has a huge population. Despite this, there may be significant dangers ahead. China is still a communist country. The government still owns or controls many of the listed and traded companies both on the Shanghai and Hong Kong exchanges. Investors are a silent partner with no recourse to protect them should the government decide to change policies. Again, the margin of safety appears to be missing.

Rather than tread the savannahs of the African interior, or the steppes of Siberia, or even the slopes of the Andes Mountains, more than sufficient profits are available if I mostly stick to stable economies with stable governments. This includes all of Western Europe, Japan, Canada, New Zealand, Australia, Singapore, and non-Chinese companies in Hong Kong. In these stable, mostly democratic, and capitalist nations, I continue to look for stocks that hold the same characteristics of value as do U.S. companies.

## Chapter Eight

# Watch the Guysin the Know

*Buy when the insiders buy.*

Moving back to the United States, a leading indicator of whether the fortunes of a company are about to turn for the better can be found by watching for insider purchases. Senior management and directors are usually the first to know that operations are improving and earnings may be rising. If they begin to buy stock in the open market, it is a safe bet that things are getting better. Company employees from senior management on down, often buy and sell shares in the companies where they work (except that they may not do so during lock up periods before earnings are reported or if they are aware of non-public information). Regulations exist to prevent insiders from unloading shares onto the public before bad news is released. But the regulation that benefits us the most is not one that prevents company insiders from selling but the one that requires that all transactions be reported within two business days. Any time an insider buys or sells stock, it is public information within 48 hours. This allows us to invest our money very close to the same time that the people running the company decide to invest theirs.

There are a lot of reasons insiders may sell shares in their company. They may wish to diversify their holdings, plan their estate, buy a dream house, or pay off a soon-to-be ex-spouse. They may sell shares obtained by exercising stock options. For these reasons, sales by insiders are not as strong an indicator as their buys. There is only one logical reason for insiders to reach into their wallets and buy stock in the open market. They think the stock price is going higher. I pay close attention to insider buying because these people have intimate knowledge of the business and the prospects for improvement in current conditions. They run the company. They often have insights into new marketing programs, improving industry conditions, undervalued assets held by the company, and the potential for future financial transactions that improve the health of the business. If they think business is about to get better or the stock is underpriced, it makes sense to investigate further.

Not only does this conclusion make perfect sense, once again extensive research bears it out. Stocks bought by insiders outperform the market by at least a two-to-one margin, and this applies around the world (unfortunately, only a few countries outside the United States require company insiders to report their stock purchases and sales). Insider buying of stocks selling at low multiples of earnings or below asset value is even better. Consistent purchases by insiders is an even better indication—with below-book-value stocks. And, you guessed it, stocks with high valuations and insider selling tend to underperform by a wide margin.

There is another way that corporate insiders can send a signal that better times may be ahead. When the board of directors of a company decides to buy back its stock in the open market, it may well be a sign that they believe the shares are undervalued and do not adequately reflect the future prospects for growth. They feel that the best return on corporate cash is by buying up their own shares in the marketplace. If they are correct and are buying the shares at a discount to what they are worth, then per share value for other shareholders increases. Any share buybacks done below book value will increase the per share book value of the remaining shares. With so many potential benefits from a share buyback, it makes sense to look closely at companies announcing stock buybacks that appear to be cheap relative to earnings or assets.

Corporate insiders, whether spending their own or the corporation's money, usually make a significant statement when they buy shares in the companies they run. Insiders are usually investors, not traders. They tend to buy for the long term, not the short term. Many research studies verify that insider buying and share buybacks tend to occur in stocks with a low price compared with earnings, a low price-to-book value, and a price that has fallen quite a bit. In other words, insider purchases are often a signal to the kinds of companies we seek for the shelves of our value investing store because they often have the other traits that make them strong candidates.

There is another type of insider that we should look for. Investors who accumulate 5 percent or more of a company's shares must file with the Securities and Exchange Commission and make public information about their holdings. They must also state whether they bought the shares purely as an investment or if they intend to lobby for changes or seek control of the company. Many of these larger investors have successful track records, and it's worth noticing if they have a large position in a stock that appears undervalued. Knowing that very successful investors are interested is a reason for us also to take a look.

The activist investors who are looking to influence or change management are also worth tracking. Shares of Six Flags Amusement Parks posted large gains after the owner of the Washington Redskins, Daniel Snyder, expressed an interest in the theme park operator. Time Warner, Wendy's, and HJ Heinz have all come under pressure from outside investors to improve results and increase returns for shareholders. Not all the activist investors are successful, but their presence offers us one more screen for value opportunities. They act as another influence on the management of an undervalued stock to increase value or risk losing their jobs. If the stock is already selling at a low price to earnings or assets, then the presence of a successful activist may give us a strong reason to take a look.

Sometimes the only thing standing in the way of a cheap stock and a profit for an investor is a catalyst that can make the market take notice. Both insider buying and activist investors can provide the push that makes the market realize a stock is a good value.

## Chapter Nine

# Things That Go Bumpin the Market

*Falling prices can be a double-edged sword.*

When children hear strange noise in the night, they tend to imagine all sorts of scary things—ghosts, monsters, and frightening creatures lurking under the cloak of darkness. Bumps in the night send children running down the hall in search of the comfort of their parents' bedroom. The monsters may be imaginary, but they seem all too real to a child. The child's fears are not rational and the panicky flight down the hall is a gross overreaction. Amazingly enough, adult investors, both individuals and so-called professionals, act the same way when things go bump in the market. We have seen markets fall time and again because of some political or economic announcement. Likewise, individual stocks and sectors often fall on weaker than expected earnings or unforeseen events. As prices fall, at exactly the time investors should be sharpening their pencils to select stocks to buy at lower prices, they join the panic and run down the hall for the unreasonable security of a cash position. Risk is more often in the price you pay than the stock itself.

I have seen many market sell-offs over the span of my career, including major declines such as the 1972 to 1974 bear market caused by higher oil prices and a stag-flated economy, the crash of 1987, the minicrash of 1989 and the high-yield bond debacle that followed, the Asian flu culminating in a brief panic in the United States in 1998, and the 2001 to 2002 market implosion. In each case, the rapid decline of prices brought bargain issues that an investor could buy for a lot less than their precollapse price. As others around you are selling in reaction to news reports, you can load up the shelves of your store with value opportunities that can benefit from the subsequent price recoveries. It is important to understand that the prices of solid companies with strong balance sheets and earnings usually recover. In my experience, if the fundamentals are sound, they always have and they always will.

As with the other characteristics that are sources of value opportunities for the shelves of our store, there has been an enormous amount of research into the results achieved by buying markets, stocks, countries, and sectors that have gone bump in the night. From 1932 to nearly the present, the studies confirm that when bad things happen to good companies, they recover—and usually quite nicely in a reasonable amount of time. It has also been shown that high performance seems to beget lower returns, and low performance leads to higher returns in nearly all markets from the United States and Canada to Japan and Europe (see "Don't Take My Word for It"). Today's worst stocks become tomorrow's best stocks, and the darlings of the day turn into tomorrow's spinsters.

There is danger in trying to catch a falling knife, as the saying goes on Wall Street, but even when stocks dropped 60 percent in one year, and bankruptcy and failure rates jumped fourfold, opportunities abounded. Remember that one of the chief tenets of the value investing approach is to always maintain a margin of safety. You can lessen the chances of buying a failure and increase your portfolio performance if you stick to the principle of margin of safety. Don't try to catch an overpriced, cheaply made falling knife.

The studies, by esteemed scholars and secretaries of the U.S. Treasury, are consistent with my experiences in the investment business. On the one hand, when stock prices fell on average some 60 percent after the bear market of 1973 to 1975 and the former market darlings—the Nifty Fifty as they were called—had collapsed even further, many investors were decimated. Warren Buffett, on the other hand, was thrilled with all the bargains he found as a result of the collapse. In an interview with *Forbes* in the November 1, 1974, issue, he described himself as feeling like an "oversexed guy in a harem" and finished the interview by saying that now was the time to invest in stocks and get rich. The average investor and many professionals, having suffered through a bear market, wanted nothing to do with stocks and missed out on the chance to load up on inventory at the lowest prices in 20 years.

During the 1980s, I saw some of the large public utilities overcommit to nuclear power with disastrous financial results. Some of the largest electric utility companies in the United States fell into financial difficulty. Many of them even had to file for bankruptcy to work out their difficulties. After the Three Mile Island accident, world interest in U.S. nuclear power practically ground to a halt. Few portfolio managers or individuals wanted to invest in these companies. But those brave few who invested in concerns like Public Service New Hampshire, Gulf States Utilities, and New Mexico Power ended up with enormous returns over the balance of the decade as the companies worked out their problems and returned to profitability.

In the late 1980s and early 1990s, the fall of Drexel Burnham, the junk bond powerhouse, and the implosion of the high-yield debt market, along with collapsing real estate prices, caused what is now known as the savings and loans crisis. This crisis spread from the smaller S&Ls to the largest banks in the country. Venerable institutions such as Bank of America and Chase Manhattan Bank fell to prices at or below their book value and had price-to-earnings ratios in the single digits. Wells Fargo was hit particularly hard because it appeared to have significant exposure to a rapidly declining California real estate market. Investors who did their homework and invested in banks during this time earned enormous returns over the decade that followed as the industry went though a merger boom that generously rewarded shareholders. You just had to catch the babies being thrown out with the bathwater.

After Bill Clinton took office in 1992, he appointed his wife Hillary to head a committee on health care reform that proposed a drastic program that would have dramatically curtailed the profits of the pharmaceutical industry. All the leading drug company stocks declined sharply. Companies like Johnson &

Johnson, which not only makes prescription drugs but also consumer products such as Band-Aids and Tylenol, fell to a level of just 12 times earnings. Most investors shied away from the industry. Investors who saw the opportunity in Johnson & Johnson realized that the stock was selling for the equivalent value of the consumer products side of the business. You got the prescription pharmaceutical part of J&J for free. Once Hillary care was a dead issue, the stock of J&J and the other pharmaceutical companies brought outsized gains to investors willing to take the plunge.

American Express is another example of how catching the right falling knife can sharpen returns with high-quality inventory at low prices. After the disaster of 9/11, the company was viewed as being too dependent on air travel, and its shares fell from the previous year's high of $55 to as low as $25. While travel is a big part of its business, an astute investor realized that the American Express card is also used at gas stations, supermarkets, and even Wal-Mart. Prior to the events of

September 11, card issuance had been rising, and the company had undertaken significant cost-cutting measures. Although American Express may have been facing some travel-related struggles, it was an enormously profitable company that sold at just 12 times earnings. Investors who realized that companies of this quality are rarely this cheap and that the income stream from the credit card business offered a margin of safety have been amply rewarded in the years since.

In the halls of academia, under the eyeshades of researchers, and in the rough-and-tumble world of Wall Street, buying stocks that have fallen in price and yet still offer a margin of safety has resulted in successful investments. Although the public at large and most institutional portfolio managers find it difficult to leave their comfort zone and buy stocks that have fallen, those of us buying cheap inventory realize that the bargains are found in the sales flyers and the new low lists, not in highfliers and $12 per pound Delmonico steaks.

## Chapter Ten

# Seek and You Shall Find

*Uncover treasures the modern way.*

Finding cheap stocks is a little bit like a treasure hunt. Just as the miners in the days of the California gold rush had to sift through a lot of dirt and rock to find the precious metal that would make them rich, investors have to sift through a lot of data to find the gems that will be good investments. The miners needed picks, shovels, and pans—their tools of the trade. In much the same way, investors need tools to sort through the universe of thousands of stocks listed around the world. As we try to fill the shelves of our value investing store with appropriate goods, we need to review all the available merchandise to determine which ones look like good candidates.

When I started in the investment business, sifting through the universe of stocks was a time-consuming, tedious task. I had to go page by page through the monthly *Standard & Poor's Directory of Corporations* and parse for their net current assets per share. Net current assets per share was one of Benjamin Graham's favorite measures of value. He would start with the current assets on a company's balance sheet: all the cash, inventory, and receivables from customers, the assets that he thought could be sold in a relatively short period. Then he would subtract from the current assets everything the company owed. If there was anything left, he divided that by the number of shares outstanding to come up with the net current assets per share. If the stock was selling for two-thirds or less of net current assets, he bought it. A pretty simple calculation but it was drudge work of the highest order. In a similar way, I plowed through *Polk's Bank Directory*, a one-foot-thick, purple-covered directory of every bank in the country. And there were a lot of banks. In those days, there was no such thing as interstate banking. Each state was a protected territory for local banks of which there were thousands. Illinois was the worst. It did not even allow branch banking, so every bank in that state was a separate company. Going through Illinois alone took four months. My assignment was to calculate the book value of every publicly traded bank in the United States. Once I had calculated book value, I would compare it with the stock price. If the stock was selling for two-thirds or less of book value, we would try to buy some. Not very sophisticated, but we bought a lot of banks on the cheap.

Eventually, databases that gathered all the annual and quarterly report information of public companies came into being. Compustat was probably the first. In the early 1980s, we would call Compustat and have it run a screen of all publicly traded companies in the United States based on criteria we thought would be useful: price-to-book value, price-to-earnings ratios, and price-to-net current assets. All still pretty rudimentary. But it was a start. It was sort of like when cars evolved to having ignitions instead of cranks to get them going.

Today we can use search engines that screen the entire world to find investment candidates that fit our criteria. We prefer Bloomberg, to which you must subscribe, but there are others on the Internet. Several of them such as Yahoo! Finance, Zacks.com, and MSN, are completely free. With just a few key strokes, you can obtain lists of all the stocks that possess one or more of any criteria you choose. With another click, you can sort them from high to low depending on which criterion you think is the most important. You can mix and match criteria, and in a matter of moments your computer will show all the lists of possible candidates for your investment store. As I sit here writing this, I can go to the screen at Zacks.com and find that as of this moment there are 751 stocks that sell below book value, that another 752 appear to be inexpensive based on earnings, and that 96 companies have fallen over 50 percent in price in the first three months of this year. A few more clicks of the mouse, and I can see that in the past three months, 209 companies have had significant buying activity by insiders and officers. This is just a list of possible candidates. Countless sites on the Internet offer prescreened lists of stocks that appear to offer value. There are also sites that focus on identifying companies that have heavy or persistent buying of shares by insiders. The combination of Moore's law about producing ever faster and more powerful computers and the expansion of the Internet have made the search for value much easier than when I started in the investment business. There is still more work to do, but we can accomplish in minutes what used to take days or weeks.

Much as the supermarket sends out sales flyers every week to let you know what is on sale, so does the stock market. This information is published every day in the *Wall Street Journal, Investor's Business Daily,* the *Financial Times,* and any number of local newspapers. On the Internet, *Barron's* publishes a list of new weekly lows every Saturday. These lists of new lows are good starting points in the search for value.

Screening for stocks that seem cheap on the surface is only a beginning. Blindly buying the new low list or the screen results could well end in investment disaster. These names are just a list of possible candidates for the shelves of our wealth-building store. We still need to examine the merchandise to make sure we are being offered quality goods at low prices and not shabby obsolete articles that are hopelessly overpriced even while appearing to be cheap. With more than 20,000 public companies worldwide to choose from, only a superman version of Evelyn Wood's speed reading tactics could get through all the annual reports. The screens and the new low lists point us in the direction of potentially cheap stocks, and reduce the number of companies we need to study with greater care. Every great corporate disaster would have appeared on the new low list—Enron, WorldCom, all the Internet busts of 2002 would have shown up on one or more of these lists. Because maintaining a margin of safety is one of the core principles of wealth building through value investing, our lists are a starting point, not a destination.

A savvy store owner will visit competitors to see what they stock on their shelves, what is selling well in their location, and what seems to be worthless inventory. As we build our inventory of value opportunities, we can do the same and observe what other value investors are doing. It is a fairly easy task using mutual fund-ranking services such as Morningstar. All managers must file a report of all stocks, bonds, and other securities in their portfolio at least twice a year. This is a gold mine of helpful information. These will be lists of stocks that the very best investors think are good opportunities for building wealth. As we look over these lists, we can find ideas that we may have overlooked in our search for inventory, or verify that stocks on our lists may be worth further consideration. Some of the names that have been in the portfolio for a long time may have appreciated significantly and are no longer value opportunities for us. Some, however, will be newer inclusions and may be available at around the same price that the best of the best acquired their shares. The manager reports also include the letters to shareholders, and these letters give us insight into the current thinking of the managers and their outlook for the stocks they own and the markets in general. With just a few mouse clicks, you have immediate insight into the portfolios and current thinking of some of the best value investors.

Once we have found some names that the best value investors have purchased, we can go one step farther. By going to one of the various Internet financial and investing sites such as Yahoo! we can see who else owns the stock. Among these names will be some managers not covered by Morningstar such as hedge fund managers or private investment managers. Here is a whole new list of value portfolios worth investigating as we search for opportunities to stock our shelves.

Another method for uncovering opportunities that might belong in our inventory is to look at the prices paid in corporate mergers and acquisitions to find stocks that are selling at a significant discount to what they are actually worth to a knowledgeable buyer. This discount will not escape the eyes of a competitor or larger corporation that might have an interest in entering a particular industry by taking over a company in that field. Most of the time, mergers or takeovers will occur at a price that is fairly close to the real worth of the business. The swarms of investment bankers, accountants, and lawyers climbing all over these deals with pencils and spreadsheets see to that. Looking at other companies in the same industry and comparing the price they sell at when measured against earnings, assets, or sales volume may well help us uncover companies that sell at a discount to their takeover value and are worthy of consideration. It is a fairly simple task to look at other companies in fields where merger activity is brisk and compare other companies' values against what is being paid by fairly knowledgeable buyers. Savvy value investors can collect the prices paid in acquisitions, calculate the financials including price to sales, price to EBIT (earnings before interest and taxes), the pretax, pre-interest earnings, and EBITDA (earnings before interest, taxes, depreciation, and amortization), along with other ratios, and keep them in a proprietary database for future reference like I do.

Whether screening financial databases or watching what other smart investors are buying, you are looking for clues to hidden value. With more than 20,000 publicly traded companies in the world, it is impossible to investigate each one. You have to search for markers much like tracking a deer through the woods. Once you know which markers are most likely to lead to an investment opportunity, your hunt for value becomes much easier.

## Chapter Eleven

# Sifting Out the Fool's Gold

*When is a bargain not a bargain?*

Once we have assambled a list of likely candidates, we have to determine which to put into our inventory of companies bought cheaply and which to tell politely, "no, thank you" and move on. Many of the companies on our initial list are cheap for a reason; they have fundamental problems that make them decidedly not valuable. At various times in the past few years, names like Enron, Global Crossing, MCI, U.S. Airlines, and Pacific Gas and Electric might have popped up on a list of value candidates whose stock price had fallen significantly. However, these companies ended up filing for bankruptcy, and shareholders lost a significant portion of their investment if not all their money. To achieve our wealth-building goals, we have to determine why a company's shares are cheap and which ones have little chance of recovery.

The first and most toxic reason that stocks become cheap is too much debt. In good times, companies with decent cash flow may borrow large amounts of money on the theory that if they continue to grow, they can meet the interest and principal payments in the future. Unfortunately, the future is unknowable, and companies with too much debt have a much smaller chance of surviving an economic downturn. In recent years, companies in telecommunication and cable assumed that the good times would last forever. However, as technology changed and prices dropped due to increased competition, it became more and more difficult for them to meet those mounting interest bills. In one of Ben Graham's last interviews, he explained that he used a simple yardstick to measure health. A company should own twice as much as it owes. This philosophy has helped me avoid companies that owe too much to survive.

Stock prices may also drop, and thus make our list, because a company falls short of Wall Street analysts' earnings estimates. Analysts seem to be more focused on short-term earnings gains than future long-term success. There are literally thousands of analysts following companies around the world, and they supply this information to large institutional investors and individuals. Countless investment systems are built on the concept of buying shares when a company exceeds the analysts' estimates and selling shares when it doesn't. This thinking prevails even though quarterly or yearly earnings estimates have been proven to be notoriously unreliable. The accuracy of these numbers matters little in the calculation of the analysts' compensation; rather analysts are paid based on the commission dollars generated for their firm in stocks they cover. Routinely, large and good companies get pushed to new stock price lows because they missed the estimates of the thundering herd of Wall Street. Missing earnings is not fatal, and it tends to create opportunity for the value buyer; if the trend continues, however, the shares will likely continue to fall.

Some cyclical stocks may show up on our list of potential bargains. By this, I mean that they are highly dependent on how the economy is doing. While everyday purchases like food, soap, diapers, and the like are unlikely to be put off because times are slow, buying a new car or a new washing machine or even a new house may well be delayed if the economy slows. As a result, industries like automobiles, large appliances, steel, and construction will experience lean times and stock prices are likely to reflect this fact. Although we have had recessions of varying lengths and depths, the economies of industrialized nations have always rebounded. It is important to note that in the bad times, cyclical companies with heavy debt loads may well face insurmountable problems. Adhering to a policy of avoiding overly leveraged companies will serve you well.

Stocks may also fall because of labor contracts. During good times, some companies and industries cave into labor union demands that were affordable at the time. Little did they realize that they were mortgaging their future. As new competition unburdened by costly labor contracts enters their industries, their profits disappear. Think about the Big Three auto companies or the major airlines. In many cases, the unions have been unwilling to grant concessions. It is never easy to give back something you have, even if not doing so threatens the very existence of the company you work for. Although holding on to expensive contracts may or may not benefit management or the unions in the long run, the one person that most assuredly does not benefit is the stockholder. Another problem facing old-line industrial companies is unfunded pensions. Many large corporations have pension liabilities—benefits promised to workers—that they simply will be unable to pay. Generally speaking, if a company has excessive pension liabilities or there exists a contentious labor environment, it may be best to put these companies' shares on the no-thank-you list.

Increased competition is yet another reason for falling share prices. Highly profitable industries attract new competition. The most serious form of this comes when an industry in one country has high-priced labor or expensive regulatory rules. Other nations unburdened by such costs can often produce and export the same goods cheaper. Think China. It is simply a hard fact of life that we live in a global economy and if goods and services can be provided at a lower price, people and companies will buy at the lower price. Throughout the world, countries have seen foreign manufacturers of automobiles, appliances, and other goods make significant inroads into their market. Virtually no electronic consumer products are still manufactured in the United States even though the vast majority of these products were invented there. Being patriotic is one thing. Paying twice as much for a product that you can get from someplace else at a much lower price goes against human nature. If a company is facing strong competition from a more efficient competitor with lower costs, it is perhaps best to utter those comforting words "no, thank you" and move on to the next candidate.

Obsolescence is another potentially fatal cause for falling prices. Although I am sure that the last largescale manufacturer of buggy whips or hand-cranked automobile starters made a very fine product, there was simply no longer a need for its product. When was the last time you bought a set of rabbit ears for a TV set or an antenna for your house? There may be some small demand for these products, but a company that depended on them for most of its sales would soon be out of business. Consider the field of technology. The rate of "creative destruction" has never been faster. Newer and better products turn up every day making the older products obsolete. The new products are a boon to the consumer but the bane of the legacy company. Will we need a chain of Blockbuster Video stores once we can download over the Internet any movie ever made? Today, you can go online and order any movie from NetFlicks and never have to leave the comfort of your own home. Who needs to pay Verizon $99 per month for phone service when you can sign up with Vonage for $29 per month? For this reason, you should avoid companies that are subject to technological obsolescence. The world is simply changing too fast to depend on products and services that someone else can deliver better and for less cost.

Perhaps one of the most dangerous reasons for share price drops is corporate or accounting fraud. Although these crimes against investors are the exception and not the rule, and most CEOs are dedicated leaders who care about their companies and their shareholders, fraud does happen. In recent years, the world has experienced some of the largest cases in history. Enron, Parmalat, Tyco, WorldCom, and others have marched across our television screens in the past few years. Many of the frauds were a result of a seemingly "anything goes, just make the numbers attitude" that permeated in the boom years of the 1990s. Regulators have since done much to help prevent future occurrences, but I suspect that there will always be some form of shenanigans. Criminals exist in every walk of life. There is almost no way to uncover fraud before it becomes public. By the time it is discovered, it is too late. The best the investor can do is to steer clear of financial reports that seem overly complicated.

The best candidates are companies in industries the average Joe can understand. And, as Buffett likes to tell it, companies that are surrounded by a moat are even better. A moat can come in the form of patent protection for an essential product we need, or a brand name that has broad consumer recognition. Moats tend to scare off competition. Moats also come in the form of size. Does anyone think they could start a business that could compete with the likes of a Wal-Mart? There will always be competition, and no moat lasts forever. But a moat can permit a company to make significant profits for many years.

I like to stick to businesses we understand and for which there is an ongoing need. Banking is a prime example. Once man evolved from being a nomadic hunter and gatherer, he needed a bank. Banks are perhaps the oldest industry after the oldest profession, and no one has yet invented something better. As financial assets grow, so should banks. They have also been great innovators for which they are given little credit. The average person views banks as stodgy, old economy relics. However, where would we be without ATMs, debit cards, or credit cards? Probably half the people living in the developed world today don't remember what it was like to live in a world without cash machines.

I also like food, beverage, and consumer staples like detergents, toothpaste, pens, and pencils—the stuff we consume on a daily basis. Many of these products engender brand loyalty that keeps us buying the same product day after day, week after week. If you have a favorite beer, you probably buy the same brand 90 percent of the time. Likewise everything from tissue paper to spaghetti sauce. We are all creatures of habit, and we will usually repeat our consumer preferences when we go shopping.

I approach my list of investment candidates with a healthy dose of skepticism. My best friend in the whole world when it comes to building my inventory of value investing opportunities is the no-thank-you pile. If there is something you do not understand or are not comfortable with, in the no-thank-you pile it should go. If a company has too many problems—too much debt, union and pension problems, stiff foreign competition—on the pile it goes. I have the luxury of filling my store with merchandise I am comfortable with and want to own for the long-term wealth building it offers.

## Chapter Twelve

# Give the Companya Physical

*A thorough checkup will help avoid investing mistakes.*

Now that we have a list of candidates and have determined the reasons the stock is cheap, it is time to figure out what the company is actually worth. Start by examining the balance sheet. Much as a doctor consults patients' charts to see what condition they are in, look to the balance sheet to see what shape the company is in. The doctor needs to know all the vital signs to make a diagnosis. A balance sheet is effectively a company's medical chart, a snapshot of its financial condition at a given point in time. It shows how solvent the company is and exactly what shape—good or bad—it is in. Here is where you begin to develop a better idea of what the company is actually worth, how much it owes, and what resources it has to survive going forward. The balance sheets show what assets can be quickly converted to cash, and what fixed assets like factories and equipment are owned. The balance sheet also tells how much money the company owes and its net worth. It is basically the same form you fill out when you apply for a loan.

One of the most important aspects of the balance sheet is liquidity. Liquidity is the amount of cash the company can lay its hands on in the short term. Liquidity provides the flexibility to withstand down cycles in the economy, pay dividends to shareholders, buy back stock, and take advantage of future opportunities. You also want to make sure that the company is not overly burdened with debt, and that there is enough capital to stay in business during bad times.

The first place to look on the balance sheet is the category of current assets. Here the company lists all its cash and assets that can be turned into cash in a relatively short period such as a year or less. This includes shortterm investments such as T-bills, inventories that are finished products ready for sale or products that are in the process of being manufactured, and receivables from customers who have bought their products.

Next is the current liabilities section of the balance sheet. As current assets are assets that can generally be converted to cash in a year or less, current liabilities are debts that fall due within a year or less. They include such items as interest payments on the company borrowings and accounts payable to the company's suppliers, as well as taxes owed but not yet paid. Dividing current liabilities into current assets gives us an important ratio in balance sheet analysis, the current ratio. This ratio reveals a company's ability to pay its short-term obligations. A rough rule of thumb is a ratio of two to one, that is, the company has twice the amount of liquid assets as it has short-term debts and obligations. This can vary depending on the business, but I like to err on the conservative side. It is also helpful to compare this number to other companies in the same industry. By comparing companies in the same industry, the investor can then determine which companies are in better financial shape. When compared against the industry average, a lower ratio may indicate possible liquidity problems. It is also important to look at the ratio over the past several years. A current ratio that is steadily declining year over year may indicate that a serious liquidity problem is developing. It is also helpful to examine the relationship in cash terms. When you subtract the current liabilities from the current assets, you have calculated what is known as working capital. The rule of thumb here is simply the more the better. It is also a good idea to see if this number is rising or falling over the years. A variation of the current ratio, known as the quick ratio, removes inventory from the calculation. Although inventory can usually be converted to cash, it may be impossible for the company to receive full value for inventory if it is subject to a fire sale. This is also sometimes called the *acid test ratio* and gives a clear view of a company's cash position versus its bills.

It is also a good idea to track inventory levels over the past several years to see if they have been steadily rising in relationship to the company's sales. Rising inventories may indicate a product that has decreased in popularity and will be difficult to sell at a profit.

Next, look at the company's long-term assets and debts. Long-term assets include real estate, factories, warehouses and equipment, and investments in subsidiaries or stocks that it has no intention of selling. Intangible assets such as patents, trademarks, or copyrights are also listed as long-term assets. I tend to take these assets out of my calculations as their value may be difficult to determine. The value of intangible assets should be reflected in the company's earnings, which we will get to later.

Once I have an idea of how much the company owns, I turn to what it owes. Long-term liabilities include all debt that is due longer than one year from now. This includes bank loans, public and private bond issues, and long-term leases for property or equipment. Again, it is useful to observe trends over the past few years. Are liabilities growing faster than assets? This could be an indication that the company has to borrow more and more money just to stay afloat. Likewise, a situation where long-term debt is declining year over year while assets are rising indicates that the company is generating excess cash and using it to pay down debt, a healthy indication for the years ahead.

When I subtract all that the company owes from all that it owns, I get shareholder equity, or book value. This final book value is simply a more detailed form of the value discussed in Chapter 5. It is the ultimate measure of how equity has built up over the years both from money raised and earnings retained and reinvested in the business. Again, I prefer to subtract intangible assets from this number to get a better picture of how much actual equity there is in a company that could potentially be realized if needed.

Another measure that gives us a good idea of a company's solvency and ability to survive is the debt-to-equity ratio. This is the total debt, both long and short term, divided by the shareholder equity. If the number is higher than one, we know that the company is funded primarily by debt rather than equity investment. This is not necessarily the end of the world, but it means you need to investigate further. It pays to compare this number with that of other companies in the same industry. A stable business such as a public utility can service more debt than a young technology company that needs cash to reinvest in research and development of new products. In general, a high debt-to-equity ratio means that a company has been financing its growth by borrowing. Leveraging the company by increasing debt levels is a double-edged sword. If a company can invest the money it borrows, and earn a higher return than it pays in interest, it should be able to quickly improve its profits. If it cannot earn a higher return than the interest it pays, there is a real danger of default and bankruptcy down the road. The less debt on the balance sheet, the greater the margin of safety.

The balance sheet is the starting point. You are primarily looking for red flags that may tip you off that the company has more serious problems than you originally thought. Evaluating not only the levels of debt, assets, and working capital but the trends in each can give you valuable information about the company's health and future prospects. Comparing the leverage ratios of a company with others in the same industry also indicates its competitive position and its ability to ride out adverse economic times.

It is here that you begin to understand how solid the book value of a company is. Recall that a low price-to-book-value ratio is one characteristic of a winning stock. If the book value of a company contains a lot of intangible assets like goodwill, or excessive inventory in relation to its sales, it may not be quite the bargain we thought. Sometimes, however, you may find that the book value is understated. Land or stock investments acquired years earlier may be carried on the balance sheet at cost. These assets may have appreciated over the years, and the stock may be even more of a bargain than we originally thought. I have found this to be true several times over the years, particularly in foreign stocks.

Remember, winning in the investment game means not losing. A strong balance sheet is a good indicator of a company's stamina, its ability to survive when the going gets tough.

Once you have satisfied yourself that a company is resting on a solid foundation, it is time to look at its earnings prospects.

## Chapter Thirteen

# Physical Exam, Part II

*The stock checks out okay, but what can it earn?*

Once you are satisfied that a company is on firm financial ground with a strong balance sheet, it is time to examine the income statement. The income statement is simply a record of how much money the company took in over a period of time (its sales or revenues) and how much it paid out (its expenses) over the same period. Most companies report income on both a quarterly and an annual basis. The annual income statement is more useful because some companies experience seasonal sales fluctuations. Retailers in particular see large swings, as a significant part of their business occurs around the yearend holidays. Remember, the prices of the vast majority of stocks are driven by earnings.

The first line of the income statement is the company's sales or revenues. These terms are interchangeable. In general, service companies have revenues, and manufacturing companies have sales. Revenues or sales are the lifeblood of the company. Without them, a company can't earn a profit. While revenues in any given year are important, they only have meaning when compared with previous years. Most company annual reports show revenues and earnings for the past five years. A look at the top line revenue growth gives us an idea of how the business is progressing. Revenues growing over time are good. Conversely, declining revenues may be a cause for concern. In addition, many companies have different divisions making different products, and break out revenues by division or product line. It can be helpful to see exactly where the revenues are coming from. A particularly well-performing division may be masking problems in a company's core business. Conversely, a particularly poorly performing division may hide the overall strength of the core business. This is true both for revenues and net income.

Having analyzed the revenue line, now turn your attention to the expense side of the ledger. First comes the cost of goods sold. This is the direct cost of producing whatever product or service the company sells. It includes the raw material and manufacturing/labor cost of making the company's product. This number can fluctuate over time. If it is rising as a percentage of revenues, it may indicate that rising costs that cannot be passed on to the customer are squeezing the long-term potential for profits. Or the number can indicate that the company faces new competition that may also squeeze profits. Sometimes higher expenses may indicate softening demand that may or may not be due to cyclical effects. Companies often discount the price of their products to move inventory off the shelf.

After deducting the cost of goods sold, you arrive at the gross profit. The percentage of gross profit divided by sales is the gross profit margin. I like for this to be a fairly stable number, but often it is not. It tends to fluctuate with demand for the company's products or services. The steadier the gross profit margin, the better the business. From the gross profit margin, we now subtract operating expenses (called "selling, general and administrative expenses") in the income statement. These are all those fixed expenses like the headquarters and all those employees who are not directly involved in producing whatever the company sells. The lower this number is as a percentage of sales, the better. A high or growing level of operating expenses could indicate bloated salaries or a less than watchful eye on overall expenses. Once you have this figure, you have the operating profit, or earnings before interest and taxes. This is the number that I like to use in valuing a company, as it is the figure most likely to be used by anyone interested in acquiring the entire company.

Interest expense, taxes, and depreciation are subtracted from operating profit to derive the final earnings for the time period. Depreciation reflects the loss of value of fixed assets such as the company's buildings, machinery, and equipment as they wear out. One other line is frequently added or subtracted from the operating profit, and it should be investigated rather closely. A company that appears to sell for six or seven times earnings may have earnings grossly inflated by a large one-time gain from the sale of a subsidiary or real estate. Since such one-time events are unlikely to occur every year, the onetime gain needs to be taken out. These are extraordinary items that do not recur with any predictability. There may also be extraordinary losses, such as expenses incurred in closing down a money-losing division that will not have any recurring effect on the company's ongoing operations. You might determine that earnings will be higher next year without these losses and the shares may be even cheaper than you first thought.

Now that you have a bottom line net profit number after accounting for all expenses, you can calculate the earnings per share that is used in measuring the stock. This is net profits divided by the number of shares outstanding. This gives you the earnings per share for the company. Simple, right? Well, not exactly. Many companies have granted options to executives that may be converted into stock, or have issued bonds, preferred stock, or warrants that can be converted into shares. For that reason, you must also calculate the diluted earnings per share (EPS) if all convertible instruments were converted into stock. A number here that is very low compared with the original EPS is a warning sign that perhaps the shares are not as cheap as they first appeared. Again, I like to use the earnings before interest and taxes to determine both regular and fully diluted earnings per share numbers. In my opinion, it is a more accurate measure of corporate earning power.

The most revealing aspect of the income statement is the trend over 5 or 10 years. Are revenues rising or falling? Are expenses staying in line with revenues? Are profits consistent or uneven? Is there a cyclical pattern to earnings such as would be the case with economically sensitive companies? Are profits growing? Are there a lot of one-time charges or gains that indicate the company may be manufacturing or massaging the bottom line? I also look closely at the shares outstanding. A rising number may indicate that excessive stock options are being granted to executives, and this will dilute my share of corporate profits. Increasing shares outstanding can also indicate that the company is financing itself through stock offerings rather than earnings. A declining number indicates that the company is actively buying its own shares, which, as discussed in Chapter 8, is usually a good sign. But watch to see that the company walks its talk. Sometimes a company may announce its intention to buy back stock but never actually makes the purchases. In the income statement, I can see if the shares outstanding are actually falling on a year-to-year basis.

Once you have a fair picture of a company's earnings, you can focus on other important ratios. One of the more important ratios I like to look at is *return on capital* (ROC). This is calculated by dividing earnings in any given year by the beginning year's capital, stockholder equity plus debt. This is a good measure of how much money a company can earn on the capital it employs. A company with a high return on capital has a much greater chance of financing growth with self-generated cash than one with a low return. Again, you should be mindful of the trends. At a minimum, I like to see stability. This indicates that management is doing an adequate job of investing and managing the reinvested profits each year. A rising ROC would tell me that they are doing a fantastic job of reinvesting profits. Conversely, a declining ROC, especially on a consistent basis, might indicate that management is not really growing the business and reinvesting at the same level of profitability. The ideal company needs more capital that it can reinvest in its business at a high rate of return. Far too often, this is not the case. Often, every dollar of earnings reinvested in the business earns a lower return than the previous dollar. In the 1980s, Philip Morris was one of the most profitable companies in the United States, but because it was in the politically incorrect business of selling cigarettes, it sold for only nine times after tax earnings. (I will refrain from making any value judgments on the cigarette business here.) Philip Morris could not reinvest its earnings in the cigarette business because it was simply too profitable and did not need new investment. So the firm launched a series of acquisitions of food companies, presumably to recast itself in a better light. It bought General Foods for approximately 15 times earnings and Kraft Foods for nearly 20 times earnings. Wasn't their own stock a better deal at 9 times earnings? Wouldn't the shareholders of Philip Morris have been better off with the company buying in its own shares or paying out generous dividends?

It is also important to consider the net profit margin. This is simply the earnings divided by the total revenues. If a company can grow its profit margins over time, every new dollar of goods sold has a leveraged impact on sales. Again, at a minimum, I like to see a consistent profit margin over a span of time. Investors who paid close attention to net profit margins could have predicted that the price wars in telecommunications, computers, and autos over the past few years were going to negatively impact earnings, and they could have exited the stocks before prices collapsed. A falling margin could also indicate bloated overhead and careless management, or cutthroat competition, something we very much want to avoid as we stock the shelves of our store.

Analyzing an income statement may seem difficult at first. It need not be. Once you have a basic understanding of what you are looking for in all the numbers, it becomes a relatively simple task to make the important calculations and comparisons. If you cannot understand a company's income statement, just put that company in the no-thank-you pile instead of feeling that you are not smart enough to figure it out. A lot of reputedly smart professional analysts could not figure out Enron's income statement, but that did not stop them from becoming big fans of the stock.

Now that you have put together a list of candidates and have determined that they have strong balance sheets and earnings, it is time to put it all together and finalize your selections.

## Chapter Fourteen

# Send Your Stocks to the Mayo Clinic

*For a thorough examination, use these easy tips from a professional.*

If you really want to get under the skin of a company, really try to understand its competitive position and growth prospects, you should ask a series of questions.

Book value, cheap earnings, balance sheet analysis—all these metrics are key to identifying good prospects. But if successful investing was as simple as a mathematical formula, everyone would have nothing but winners in their portfolios. There is some art to identifying the best prospects, and so you should analyze your list of companies in greater detail. You need to drill down farther to get a better sense of how these companies operate and compete. Getting answers to these questions will give you a more in-depth knowledge of a company and its potential as a successful investment.

1. *What is the outlook for pricing for the company's products? Can the company raise prices? Each dollar of price increase will increase pretax income by $1.00 if costs do not increase.* A company with a product that is in demand can easily raise prices to generate more profit. If costs remain the same, every extra dollar will go straight to the bottom line. For years, Philip Morris could raise the price of a pack of cigarettes pretty much whenever it wanted. At one point, Harley Davidson could price its motorcycles at a premium to its competitors because demand was so strong. Technology companies, however, are in a highly competitive environment that makes it difficult to raise prices (there is another computer company around every corner ready to lower prices). The same holds true for grocery businesses. Wal-Mart puts downward pricing pressure on all its competitors because it buys in volume at lower prices, and its other costs are less because it is more efficient. Also, if demand for a product is waning in a

particular industry, no amount of good business practices will allow for price increases.

In the past few years, some events and trends have allowed certain industries to raise prices with little ceiling pressure. Homebuilders could raise prices due to everincreasing demand. Post Katrina, insurance companies raised prices as many people and businesses scrambled to buy extra disaster insurance. The less competition in an industry, the easier it is to increase prices.

2. *Can the company sell more? What is the outlook for units? A 10 percent hike in units will increase gross profits by 10 percent if the gross profit margin does not change. Pretax income will go up by this amount if other costs do not increase.* The simplest way to raise the bottom line is to sell more products or services. Assuming that costs remain about the same, every increase in the number of units sold improves the bottom line. When Johnson & Johnson sold off during the health care reform scare of the early 1990s, the underlying business conditions were not

deteriorating. An aging population was going to lead to more demand not only for prescription drugs but also for over-the-counter medicines like Tylenol. When recently looking at a uniform and protective clothing business it seemed clear that ever-increasing safety regulations for employers would push up the demand for its products.

However, it is important to make sure that increased sales are not done through incentives or giveaways. In 2005, U.S. auto companies saw booming sales but they made little if any money off the increase in revenues. The friends and family pricing programs being offered to everyone hurt profit margins. And some companies will never be able to increase sales. Look at the travel agency business. Who needs them when you can book plane tickets and hotels online?

3. *Can the company increase profits on existing sales? What is the outlook for the gross profit margin as a percentage of sales? How much is the gross profit margin expected to increase or decrease as a result of changes in price, mix of business, or the specific*

*costs that make up the cost of goods sold?* If it is not possible to sell more, is it possible to squeeze more profit out of what is already being sold? Can the company cut product costs by changing suppliers or shipping methods? Or, as in the case of ABC Ice Cream, can it change its product mix to focus on more profitable lines of business to raise its profit margin? In 2006, many of the major media companies are diversifying away from the mainline newspaper business as circulation flattens and ad sales decrease. Companies like the New York Times and the Tribune Company are looking to increase their presence in the more profitable online world to boost overall margins and revenues. Wal-Mart never hesitates to change suppliers if it will squeeze extra profit out of a particular product line.

I also keep a watchful eye out for companies that cannot control their most basic costs. Industries like trucking or the airlines have little control over fuel costs, and a cookie company cannot control the cost of sugar.

4. *Can the company control expenses? What is the outlook for*

*selling, general, and administrative costs/margin as a percentage of sales? Have there been any changes and, if so, what are they?* Is there any way for the company to cut costs not related to making the product? Are overhead, salaries, and other employee expenses out of line? Can the company close expensive or outdated production facilities? Is a new technology available that will allow it to raise its overall profit margin? Can it lay off employees to reduce overhead? Can it refinance debt at lower rates and let the savings accrue to the bottom line?

All too often, companies let expenses get out of control and it becomes necessary to make cutbacks to restore profitability. Every dollar saved, whether in the price of paper clips or health care costs, flows to the bottom line and helps to restore profitability.

5. *If the company does raise sales, how much of it will fall to the bottom line?* If sales can be grown at no additional cost, every dollar goes right to bottom line profits. If, however, a company has to hire additional salespeople, build new plants, or add

additional shipping costs to gain growth, the increased sales will not all translate into bottom line profit. As mentioned, if increased sales are based on incentives and price cuts, the percentage of profit will be low. Often the cost of gaining revenue and market share can actually cause profit margins to fall or even reduce a company's profits. This frequently happens in technology companies where the cost of gaining business may exceed the profit potential of the business. On the flip side, Wal-Mart and Harley Davidson are great examples of companies that have maintained tremendous revenue growth while holding or even increasing their pretax profit margins.

6. *Can the company be as profitable as it used to be, or at least as profitable as its competitors?* Often I will see a company where the profit margin falls well below previous levels. If this is due to a temporary problem, the company should regain its profitability. It may have stumbled due to management error, a new product that bombed in the marketplace, or expenses that temporarily got out of

control. The reason for falling profits could be external—a rise in interest rates, or as I am seeing today, rising energy or raw material costs that cut into the bottom line of many companies. Once you determine the cause, you can decide whether the problem can be fixed and profits restored to previous levels. When I find a company whose profit levels are well below the rest of the industry, I want to know what its competitors are doing differently. Can management make the changes that will let the company catch up with its peers?

7. *Does the company have one-time expenses that will not have to be paid in the future?* Often you will find situations where earnings are temporarily depressed by a one-time expense or charge. These could be costs associated with a merger or acquisition, or the closing of a factory. Other one-time charges include the costs of lawsuits such as seen with tobacco and firearms companies, or the closing of unprofitable divisions. If it is truly a one-time expense, one can assume that

earnings will return to prior levels and the stock could rise.

8. *Does the company have unprofitable operations they can shed?* Many times, as in our example of ABC Ice Cream, a company will have a division that is losing money while its main operations are making money. Perhaps a retail chain has stores that are not up to the level of the majority of stores. If these divisions and locations can be sold or closed, earnings will rise as the losses are eliminated, I have seen this many times with companies such as James Crean, a small Irish conglomerate that engaged in a wide variety of businesses. At first glance, the stock didn't appear that cheap but repeated insider buying piqued my curiosity. A closer look showed that it was selling several divisions and the ensuing proceeds would firm up the balance sheet. In 1997, the company was actually selling at just 65 percent of the then adjusted book value. In 1996, I came across a small company by the name of National Education. It had two profitable divisions and two that were losing money. Once

management made the needed changes, the stock doubled in price. Getting rid of the money-losing operations in many cases is all the catalyst a company needs to see substantial gains in the price of its stock.

9. *Is the company comfortable with Wall Street earnings estimates?* Although I rely very little on the estimates when looking for stocks or estimating their value, I like to know if management is comfortable with the earnings estimates the Street is making. If they feel they are too high or too low, I know that missing the earnings will likely cause the stock price to fall, while exceeding the estimate will often cause the price to move higher.

10. *How much can the company grow over the next five years? How will the growth be achieved?* I like to get some idea of just how much the company thinks it can grow the business over the next five years. The confidence, or lack thereof, of management in its ability to grow the business gives me a good idea of how much the stock could be expected to rise from depressed levels. I want to

know how the company intends to achieve that growth as well. Will it open new locations and enter new markets? Will it acquire other companies to grow the earnings? Will the growth come at the expense of profit margins and return on equity? I like to know that management has a plan to achieve their growth goals and has a good handle on the costs and expenses they will need to grow. Growing revenues alone is not enough if those revenues aren't generating additional profits.

11. *What will the company do with the excess cash generated by the business? Every dollar of profit not given to shareholders in the form of dividends will be retained by the company. What does management intend to do with it?* If the company is profitable and generating excess cash what is it doing with it? Does it plan to increase dividends to shareholders? Will it invest in new stores or factories? Excess cash could also be used to acquire other companies or buy back stock. I want to know what return it expects on these investments. The proper use of the excess cash flow can

add substantially to corporate earnings and increase profit in the years ahead, which bodes well for the stock price. Poor use of the money could result in falling margins and returns.

12. *What does the company expect its competitors to do?* It is simply good business practice to know, at least generally, what competitors are planning to do. The expansion plans of Lowe's have a huge impact on the results at Home Depot. The growth plans of Wal-Mart are very bad news for major grocery store chains. When one auto company decides to use incentives and rebates to spur sales, all of them have to respond in similar fashion or risk losing sales. If Pepsi introduces a wildly successful new drink concoction, Coca-Cola may have to spend some money to create a competing version or lose market share. As no man is an island, neither does any company operate in a vacuum. It has competition that is out to take away sales and profits.

13. *How does the company compare financially with other companies in the same business?* I like to see how a

company stacks up against its competition. Does the competition earn the same returns on capital? Does the company have more or less debt than its peers? If it owes a lot more money than direct competitors, the cost of servicing the debt may prevent it from keeping up in the years ahead. How does the marketplace value the company? Why does Heinz sell at 20 times earnings when Kraft sells for just 15? What do other investors see that I may be missing?

14. *What would the company be worth if it were sold?* This question has become more and more important in the day-to-day business of evaluating stocks. I first started evaluating stock selection on this basis in the 1970s when it became obvious that some television stations were selling for far less than was being paid for similar companies. The industry standard at the time was about 10 times cash flow for an acquisition, whereas I bought stock in Storer Broadcasting for just 5 times cash flow. It was eventually bought out at a large premium to the price I paid. Calculating the buyout value of stocks

became common practice. In the mid-1980s, we figured out the buyout multiples for food stocks and made several great investments in companies like General Foods. Anytime I consider a stock, I look to see at what level of earnings and book value recent takeovers and division sales have occurred.

15. *Does the company plan to buy back stock?* I look to see if the company announced a buyback and check the quarter-over-quarter shares outstanding to see if it is actually buying stock. Not all announcements of intention to buy back stock are implemented. Further, many buybacks are done just to offset stock and option grants. I want to see if there will be a real reduction of shares outstanding.

16. *What are the insiders doing?* Are insiders (company management) buying? Are they selling? I have talked about the positive impact of insider buying but selling is not always a negative. Sometimes people sell for personal reasons: They may need to pay for a onetime expense such as a new home, college education, a wedding. They may

be diversifying their estate, or paying a divorce settlement. Look for patterns. An occasional sale by an insider may mean nothing; consistent sales by many officers and directors are a clear indication that management thinks the marketplace has put too high a value on the company, and they are getting out while the getting is good.

By going through this checklist, I come away with a much better understanding of the companies that passed my initial tests for value. I can see which companies are likely to increase their stock price by growing their business and controlling expenses. I can determine the faith of management in the future of the company. The stocks that pass through these questions and have a favorable potential for growth are the ones that make their way into my portfolio.

Chapter Fifteen

# We Are Not in Kansas Anymore! (When in Rome...)

*Foreign accounting is, well, foreign.*

As we travel around the world looking for value investing opportunities, keep in mind that it's not just the language or food that is different. Accounting will be different. Although the world is moving closer to a more universal accounting system, you need to have at least some understanding of the methods you may encounter.

Accounting differences can be a problem but also an opportunity. Not only is accounting different in Europe or Asia, there are dissimilarities within Europe from one country to another. Companies in the United States keep two sets of books, one for shareholder reporting and another for tax purposes. IRS regulations may permit a company to use accelerated depreciation to provide companies with an incentive to invest more in factories and equipment. This accelerated depreciation may not reflect the useful life of the asset, so the shareholder reports will use a slower rate of depreciation that results in higher reported earnings. There is nothing illegal about this. The U.S. Tax Code is full of all sorts of incentives. In most countries in Europe, companies can only keep one set of books, so the shareholder sees the same report as the tax authorities. This can result in some interesting and valuable anomalies, as I saw with my investment in the Swiss chocolate company, Lindt and Sprungli.

When I discovered Lindt and Sprungli, the shares were trading at 12,000 SF, down perhaps 60 percent from their previous high. Earnings per share were reported as 1,121 SF for a price-to-earnings (P/E) ratio of 10.7. This was not bad for a company with Lindt's market position and in light of acquisitions of other European candy companies at multiples of pretax earnings in excess of 10 times. On closer examination, however, it appeared that some adjustments might be in order. Annual depreciation and amortization were running nearly SF 47 million on an asset base of SF 124 million or 37.7 percent per year. The assets were being depreciated every 2.6 years, which seemed a little short especially the way the Swiss build things. I looked at other candy companies. I spoke to someone at Nestlé and asked how the company looked at depreciation. I was told that Nestlé calculated depreciation as a percentage of sales, and it was among the highest at 3.5 percent. Lindt was at 6 percent of sales. The industry average was 2.5 percent, and so I chose an average of Nestlé and the industry for Lindt, or 3 percent of sales. Using 3 percent cut Lindt's depreciation in half from 46.9 million SF to 23.1 million SF, adding 23.8 million SF to pretax earnings. Taxing this additional income at the Swiss corporate rate of 35 percent increased earnings by SF 15.5 million or SF 469 per share. Adjusted earnings per share were then 1,590 SF for an adjusted P/E ratio of

7.5, which was one of the lowest P/E ratios for a major consumer franchise in the world. As you can see, while it may be an aggravation to understand accounting differences, doing so often leads to incredible opportunities.

I found numerous accounting anomalies of this sort as I researched companies in Europe. Almost uniformly, the odd accounting practices resulted in a company reporting lower earnings and lower asset values than would be the case under U.S. accounting standards. Working through the European accounting differences turned out to be a treasure hunt while sorting through accounting quirks in the United States is more like navigating a minefield. American companies are more likely to put their best face forward to their shareholders so they can justify management's bonuses and increase the value of their stock options. Only recently have European companies even had stock options, and the level of executive compensation has traditionally been much lower than in the United States. Both European and Japanese companies have traditionally been more concerned with conserving cash, which often means writing off assets faster. This practice reduces reported earnings but increases cash. Non-U.S. managements place a greater emphasis on strong balance sheets.

Trading in foreign shares used to be much more difficult. With the increased globalization of financial markets, buying and selling stocks in most developed countries is pretty much the same. Many of the larger issues around the world are listed on several exchanges including the New York Stock Exchange and NASDAQ markets in the United States. Most of the listings are in the form of securities called American Depository Receipts (ADRs). These securities were introduced to reduce the difficulties involved in buying shares in foreign countries. Right now, there are roughly 2,200 ADRs traded in the United States including such corporate giants as GlaxoSmithKline, Toyota, and Nestlé to name a few. As the stock brokerage industry has gone global, it has made it possible for virtually any brokerage firm to buy shares in foreign companies that are not listed on a U.S. exchange.

Although you may have to put forth a bit more effort to understand the differences around the world, it is worth it. The global approach to value investing provides many more opportunities to invest your money.

# Chapter Sixteen

# Trimming the Hedges

*Currencies confuse even the experts.*

Global investing presents another significant variable to investing only in U.S. stocks and that is currency. Foreign stocks are quoted in foreign currencies. While a foreign stock may rise in its quoted currency, if the currency falls in relation to your own base currency, you may lose part or all the benefit of the rising stock price. In the 1980s, until the introduction of the Euro, we had to deal with approximately 20 currencies among the developed countries of the world, and they all fluctuated vis-à-vis each other. Trying to figure what the Italian lira was going to do versus the Spanish paseta versus the U.S. dollar would have been a challenge for Einstein. Sometimes these fluctuations were mild; other times they could be dramatic. In the period from 1979 through 1984, the value of the British, French, German, and Dutch currencies declined between 45 percent and 58 percent against the dollar. Similar declines in the Standard & Poor's index would have driven investors into cash with lightning speed. Given this complexity and volatility, it makes sense to hedge your investments in foreign stocks to eliminate the effect of currency fluctuations vis-à-vis your base currency. With the introduction of the Euro in 1999, the currency problem has become much less complex. Instead of having investments spread over 20 or so currencies, you will probably have 90 percent of your investments in 4 currencies: the Euro, the British pound, the Swiss franc, and the Japanese yen.

Hedging is fairly simple. If you buy 1,000 pounds of British Tool and Die, you are not only betting on the stock, you are betting on the British pound. If the stock goes up but the pound goes down, you can lose part or all of your gain in the stock if you sell and convert your proceeds back into dollars. Conversely, if the stock goes down but the pound goes up, the rise in the currency may eliminate your loss in the stock. You can create many permutations of this exercise, and it can all get a bit confusing. However, if you hedge your investment in the 1,000 pounds that you now own by virtue of buying the British Tool and Die stock, you will only enjoy or suffer the results depending on whether the stock rises or falls in British pounds.

Here is how it works. Your investment in the stock was worth 1,000 pounds when you bought it. Since the stock is valued in pounds, you own the equivalent of that amount of currency. To eliminate the currency risk, you sell 1,000 pounds using something that is called a currency forward contract. It is like selling a stock short. You don't own the stock, you just borrow it. With the currency forward contract, you don't own the currency either, but you do own the equivalent amount in your British Tool and Die stock. You are hedged. You are long and short two instruments that are equal in value. When you sell your stock, you simply close out the contract and get paid back in dollars.

There is another school of thought on foreign currency investing. Most investors who buy foreign stocks do not hedge their currency exposure. They simply accept the added fluctuations that come with foreign stock investing and let the chips fall where they may. Long term, 10 years or more, the investment results for being hedged or not being hedged are pretty similar. Both methods have in common a choice to be currency agnostic. Either you don't want any currency effect, or you don't care. A recent study by the Brandes Institute bears this out. Results from year to year can differ significantly, but long term, the currency movements tend to cancel out. The choice is up to the investor.

What does not work is switching from a hedged to an unhedged approach depending on how you think currencies will fluctuate. Again, the Brandes study reaches the same conclusion. Those who attempt to divine currency movements have generally had poorer results than those of us who choose one method and stick with it. I have always taken the position that what I think I know how to do is analyze companies, not countries. I like to stay within my circle of competence.

## Chapter Seventeen

# It's a Marathon, Not a Sprint

*It's time in the market, not market timing, that counts.*

Many people believe that the fastest way to the highest market returns is by short-term trades that are accurately timed. If you type stock market timing into an Internet search engine, you will receive hundreds of thousands of hits. Bookstores and web sites alike are full of the holy grails of trading in stocks. How to pick bottoms, how to pick tops. They use voluminous studies, ancient mathematical ratios, and even astrology to determine when stocks are ready to advance or are in danger of falling. There are some who say that you should buy and sell based on who wins the Super Bowl. "Sell in May and go away" is often heard from those who believe that the month of the year or day of the week can predict the rise and fall of stock prices. But in more than 35 years in the investment business, I have yet to find a short-term timing strategy that works. All nature of pundits have come and gone over the years. For a short time, any of them may be right, and may make one or two amazingly accurate predictions. Eventually, all of them lose the interest of the public when the predictions prove inaccurate. I simply do not believe that there is a way to accurately and consistently time short-term market movements, and again, the research of scholars seems to bear me out.

It is simply better to be in the market, invested in the value stocks that offer the highest potential return, than to play the timing game. Between 80 and 90 percent of the investment return on stocks occurs around 2 percent to 7 percent of the time. In fact, a study by Sanford Bernstein & Company showed that from 1926 to 1993, the returns in the best 60 months, or 7 percent of the time averaged 11 percent. The rest of the months, or 93 percent of the time returns only measured around 1/100 of a percent. It strikes me as a daunting task to find a way to reliably predict the 7 percent of the time stocks do well. As a long-term investor, the real danger and threat to your nest egg is being out of the market when the big moves occur. You simply have to accept that you must endure some temporary market declines. Long-term, value investing is like flying from New York to Los Angeles. While you may encounter some air turbulence over Kansas, if your plane is in good shape, there is no reason to bail out. You will eventually reach your destination safely, and probably even on time. The same goes for investing. If your portfolio is well constructed, a bit of market turbulence is no reason to bail. You will reach your financial goals.

The reality is (and it's been proven) that the biggest portions of investment returns come from short periods of time but trying to identify those periods and coordinate stock purchases to them is nearly impossible. Two issues are at play here, both equally important: (1) short-term timing doesn't work; and (2) the highest returns are achieved by being fully invested in the market at nearly all times so that you can capture the times when stocks rise the most. You have to be in the game to win it!

Predicting short-term stock market direction, however, is a fool's game and a disservice to the investing public. Long term, the market is going up. Always has, and mostly likely always will. Market timers like to think they can capture large returns by jumping in the market to profit during periods when stocks are up, and jumping out of the market when stocks are down. This activity is not unlike the maneuvers of the driver who keeps switching lanes on the freeway when there is heavy traffic. He thinks he can pick the lane that will move fastest for the next 100 yards. Never seems to work. A mile ahead, you pass him. Market timing is the same. It may get you ahead for a brief period but you will quickly give up gains when abrupt events that could never have been predicted (such as the tragedy of 9/11, geopolitical events, and even weather cause brief downturns that are almost always followed by rising prices). You will also give up your profits to the increased costs of trading from commissions to taxes.

All manner of studies have proven, in many ways, under many scenarios, that the majority of investors buy high and sell low. Peter Lynch, the legendary and highly successful manager of the Fidelity Magellan Fund for many years, once remarked that he calculated that more than half of the investors in his fund lost money. This happened because money would pour in after a couple of good quarters and exit after a couple of not so good quarters. Nobel Prize winner William Sharpe found that a market timer must be right a staggering 82 percent of the time to match a buy and hold return. That's a lot of work to achieve what could be accomplished by taking a nap. Even worse, other research shows that the risks of market timing are nearly two times as great as the potential rewards.

Between 1985 and 2005, the annually compounded rate of return for the Standard & Poor's 500 Index was 11.9 percent. Over that 20-year period, $10,000 invested in an S&P 500 Index

Fund would have grown to $94,555. However, a recent research study concluded that the average investor only compounded at 3.9 percent over that period with $10,000 merely growing to $21,422. Why? The research paper concludes that most investors head for the hills during periods of market declines, thinking the decline will go on indefinitely. Once the market has rebounded, they return, having missed the best part of the rebound.

One of the more difficult factors in maintaining a long-term approach is that prices are so widely available. We can check the value of all of our stock holdings day by day, minute by minute. We can see how they fluctuate around short-term factors, and in many cases this information can make us a little nervous. A prime example of this is an acquaintance of mine who had a portfolio of municipal bonds worth $700,000. He was a successful commercial real estate broker who saved at least half of his earnings each year. His money was invested for the long term, and he could afford to leave it invested. But he could not stand to see the prices of stocks rise and fall each day. If he owned a stock and it closed down on a particular day, he was deeply upset. I guess he did not realize that bonds also fluctuate in price; but since he could not check their closing prices every day, he was not worried. He got his regular interest check, which he reinvested and was happy. Over the ensuing 10 years, I calculated that his municipal bond portfolio grew to $1,140,226 at an assumed interest rate of 5 percent. If the same funds had been invested in the Standard & Poor's 500 index, he would have made $2,906,639 before taxes at a 15.3 percent annually compounded rate of return. If this investment was taxed at a 40 percent rate, his after-tax nest egg would have grown to $2,023,983. His loss for not being invested in stocks was $883,757.

According to an American Century Investments study, if you had ridden out all the bumps and grinds of the market from 1990 to 2005 (through the go-go 1990s into the severe sell-off from 2000 to 2002), $10,000 invested would have grown to $51,354. If you had missed the 10 best days over that 15-year period, your return would have dropped to $31,994. If you had missed the 30 best days—one month out of 180 months—you would have made $15,730. Had you missed the 50 best days you would have come out a net loser, and your $10,000 would now be worth only $9,030.

Would you take a minute-by-minute pricing approach with anything else you own? How would you react if your house was priced every day and the quotes listed in the local newspaper? Would you panic and move if you lost 2 percent of your home's value because a neighbor didn't mow his lawn? Would you rejoice and sell if it went up 5 percent in one day because another neighbor finally painted his house? A collection of businesses bought at excellent prices is no less a long-term asset than a piece of real estate and should be treated the same way. Prices will fluctuate both up and down. What is most important is that you own the right stocks when the market does go higher. Like devotees of the lottery, you have to play to win. Using the tenets of value investing and always keeping in mind the margin of safety, the odds of winning with our approach are a bit better than playing the lottery, and it's far more remunerative than sitting on the sidelines.

The evidence is clear. It is pretty close to impossible to consistently make money market timing, and you are better off investing for the long term, riding out the bumps. Value investors have the extra security of knowing that they own stocks that have one or more of the characteristics of long-term winners and that they have paid careful attention to investing with a margin of safety.

## Chapter Eighteen

# Buy and Hold? Really?

*How should you choose between stocks and bonds?*

When people think about how to structure their portfolios, they often seek professional advice. Many times it is good; often it is not. Financial advisors are risk averse. However, their risk aversion may have less to do with your financial situation than their reputations. Conventional wisdom, the accepted standard, is that a portfolio that is invested one-third in bonds and two-thirds in stocks is the way to go irrespective of the level of your assets. The major brokerage houses issue "asset allocation" formulas depending on their view of the stock market in the near term. Sounds just like market timing to me. However, people are different. Your financial assets and your needs vary tremendously. The one-third, two-thirds formula is the standard. It is safe because that is what the herd recommends. But what if you have a gazillion dollars and need only a pittance to maintain your lifestyle? Why would you invest one-third of your money in an underperforming asset?

I admit to being an iconoclast. However, I think that the two most important considerations in formulating an asset allocation formula are age and how much money you have to support your desired lifestyle. If you are young, which I define as somewhere between 20 and 35 and have a job that pays your bills, you can take a long view on investments. My partner, John Spears, read Jeremy Siegel's *Stocks for the Long Run,* third edition, which showed that in every rolling 30-year period between 1871 and 1992, stocks as measured by an index, beat bonds or cash in every period. In rolling 10-year periods, stocks beat bonds or cash 80 percent of the time. Bonds and cash did not beat the rate of inflation over 50 percent of the time.

So why would anyone own a bond? The answer comes back to age and need. In 1987, a friend of mine asked me if I would take over managing an account he had with another money manager. I agreed, and he set the wheels in motion to transfer the account to my firm. The transfer was completed in mid-September 1987. He then told me that he would be liquidating the account at the end of that year to invest the proceeds in a real estate deal he was working on. I told him that he should liquidate the account immediately and sit on the cash. He wondered why the rush. I explained that his need for the money did not anticipate any setback in the stock market. If he could not be in for the long term, he should not be in. In late September 1987, I liquidated the account. He missed the crash of 1987, and to this day, he is convinced that I knew it was going to happen. As much as I would like to be credited with great foresight, it was no more than common sense that led to my advice. The crash of 1987 came as much of a surprise to me as it did to the rest of the world.

In the early 1980s, a longtime client sought my advice on structuring her assets. Her husband had recently passed away leaving her with a $4 million account at my firm and in addition she owned $30 million of Berkshire Hathaway stock. Her husband had been an early investor in Warren Buffett's partnership and had held on to all his Berkshire Hathaway shares. My client had always worked and previously never had need of income from her investments, but she was anticipating retiring and needed some income going forward. She had lived comfortably, but modestly, given her wealth. She calculated that she would like about $200,000 per year before taxes to maintain her lifestyle. She had consulted an accountant who had drawn up a plan that met her requirements for income, inheritance to her children, and charitable gifts. Since her Berkshire Hathaway stock had a cost basis of about $20 per share, he suggested a charitable remainder trust into which she could put the Berkshire stock, sell it without paying any capital gains taxes, and reinvest the proceeds in bonds for current income. I told her that the reason she was so rich was because all her assets had been well invested in stocks, and asked why she would want to stop enjoying the benefits of future appreciation. Based on how long her mother had lived, she was likely to go for another 35 years. Her accountant replied that she had all her assets in the stock market which was, by definition, risky. I replied that even if the stock market dropped 50 percent, she had enough money to live comfortably until the age of Methuselah. So she decided to leave everything as it was, and I would provide her income needs out the money she had invested with my firm. A number of years later, she called to review our plan. I asked her how much money she had. She said $180 million. I suggested that she leave it alone. Today I figure that she has upward of $300 million.

Another client's father died prematurely in 1947 leaving his mother $1 million, an enormous amount of money in those days. That year, my parents bought the house I grew up in for about $7,000. A Cadillac cost less than $2,000, and a year at Harvard was around $1,500. Since women had to be protected from the concerns of money in those days, his father left the money in trust with a bank. To ensure a steady income for his mother, the bank invested the estate in tax-exempt municipal bonds yielding 4 percent. An annual income of $40,000 per year in 1947 left her on easy street. However, no one thought she would live for another 45 years, which she did. When she died in 2002, she still had $40,000 per year income, but it was worth a lot less than it had been in 1947. I calculated that if her original $1 million had been invested in the S&P 500 stock index, and that if she had been allowed to spend 4 percent of the assets every year, by 1998 (the year I did this little exercise), she would have had $44 million and an annual income of $1,760,000. Fortunately, her sons were successful in their own right and were generous to her in her later years.

I went to college in the late 1960s with a number of rich kids. They had gone to exclusive prep schools in New England, lived on Park Avenue or Fifth Avenue in New York, or in grand houses outside Philadelphia or Boston, or in tony communities like Greenwich, Connecticut, or the north shore of Long Island. Having been raised in far more modest circumstances, I was a bit envious. The $7,000 house I was raised in had appreciated to $27,000 when my parents sold it 20 years later in 1967. When I started working in 1969, I would search through the proxy statements of the companies that were the source of the wealth of the rich kids from my college days. Generally, the really rich kids' dads had fortunes between $5 million and $10 million based on their stock holdings—a pretty good sum for the day, but not enough to guarantee the next generation the same lifestyle. Tax the estate by 50 percent, divide by three children, and each heir got about $1,660,000. Not bad, but not a ride on easy street. Unfortunately, many of these children not only were unlikely to inherit vast wealth, they also were not prepared for the rough-and-tumble world of raw capitalism that was about to debut in the 1980s and 1990s.

In 1976, a good friend of mine and his wife bought a grand apartment on

Park Avenue in New York. After haggling over the price for 6 months, they bought the apartment for $120,000, which was equivalent to $15 per square foot. It was an 8,000-square-foot apartment with five bedrooms, five fireplaces, and five maids' rooms. The seller was thrilled to have unloaded this white elephant, which was costing him $2,500 per month to maintain. Today, similar apartments in the same building sell for $25 million. Inflation is the slow-growing and pernicious disease that erodes wealth, and until something better comes along, stocks are the only way to keep up with inflation. While a bond will return your principal at maturity, that principal may be worth far less in terms of purchasing power when you get it.

If you don't need to tap into your nest egg to live, you can afford to take the high octane approach to investing. You can ride out any bumps along the way as you try to maximize your long-term returns. However, if your time horizon is shorter and you draw money from your nest egg to live, a bit more prudence is required. I like to think of an investment portfolio as a college endowment. Colleges take a fixed percentage out of their endowments annually to fund various programs and scholarships. Most colleges draw out 5 percent per year and invest the balance so it will grow at a rate faster than 5 percent. They hope to earn investment returns that are at least equal to or greater than the rate of inflation plus the 5 percent they are spending. This enables them to maintain the purchasing power of the endowment in perpetuity.

Individuals should structure their financial affairs in a similar way. Spend an amount you think is less than the long-term returns you think you can earn on your portfolio. Five percent is not a bad place to start. If your portfolio can grow at 10 percent, you can increase the amount you spend at the same rate as inflation. However, stock portfolios are not passbook savings accounts. Your returns will fluctuate from year to year. For this reason, I like to keep three years of spending in short-term bonds to smooth out any down years in the portfolio. Leave this money on the side and only dip into it in a year when your stocks are down. If you do this, you will not have to sell stocks when they may be cheapest to pay the rent. Stock markets can and have taken more than three years to recover to their previous high. This was definitely the case in the 1970s and is the case today. It has taken the Dow Jones Industrial Average and the S&P 500 Stock Index six years to get back near their highs of 2000. The NAS-DAQ? Forget about it. It is still way underwater. My own experience over the years is that although the broad market averages can take longer than three years to recover after a particularly nasty bear market, most value investors make up their losses in far less time. Value managers, by and large, seem to avoid the periodic market bubbles that result in painful losses.

The conventional model of portfolio construction, the one-third bonds two-thirds stocks, requires that you periodically rebalance your holdings. By this, they mean that if your stocks had a particularly great year and now are 75 percent or 80 percent of your portfolio, you should sell some stocks and invest the proceeds in more bonds. That is like selling your winners and reinvesting in your losers. How smart is that? If you already have enough cash to ride out three down years, why do you need more?

Unlike an endowment, you do not have to worry about perpetuity. But the last thing you want to do is run out of money in your old age. However, also unlike an endowment, you have to pay taxes on your gains that are not held in a tax-deferred retirement account. Portfolio rebalancing forces you to realize gains and thus pay taxes. It is important to focus on money managers and mutual funds that do not have a lot of portfolio turnover. Long-term capital gains earned on stocks held for at least a year, are taxed at only 15 percent, as are dividends. Short-term capital gains and interest income from taxable bonds are taxed at much higher rates—as high as 34 percent depending on your tax bracket. And that is before any state or local taxes.

There are several mutual funds with very low turnover. They look for stocks that are reasonably priced and that will grow over time. This is the power of compounding. Turnover is the enemy of compounding and the friend of the Internal Revenue Service. Most funds now report their gains before and after taxes. It is helpful to compare the two. If after-tax gains are significantly lower than pretax gains, it is an indication that the fund manager is making his broker happy with a lot of trades and spending your money on brokerage commissions.

A lot of what you do in investing is just simple common sense. Trying to optimize your returns by switching mutual funds or messing with your asset mix will more than likely reduce your return. Many investors think they should be proactive and keep looking for ways to tweak their investment portfolio when just sitting tight, if they made the correct choices in the first place, often would be the better course.

## Chapter Nineteen

# When Only a Specialist Will Do

*How do you pick a money manager?*

The purpose of this book has been to explain the tenets of value investing so that you can benefit from the investment strategy that has been shown to have the best long-term success. You may or may not choose the do-it-yourself route. If you have the time and the inclination to do your own investing, that is great. However, it is more important that you understand the principles of investing and know what questions to ask a possible manager or financial advisor. If you do, you can choose from the thousands of money managers for mutual funds who would be more than happy to manage your investments. Morningstar is a great service that tracks thousands of mutual funds. It breaks the funds down into style categories, shows performance, market caps, and examines the managers and explains their investment approach. Morningstar is not the final point in your search for the best money managers, but it is a good place to start.

Through the years, I have sat on the investment committees of various foundations and university endowments. I have had the opportunity to interview managers competing to manage a portion of the organization's assets. Although I have often been the one competing for accounts, sitting on the other side of the table, being the interviewer, has been instructive, if not a bit more fun than being the interviewee.

The search for a money manager usually begins with an investment style choice. An investor—individual or large endowment fund—may want to add a value manager or a growth manager, someone who invests in large caps or small caps, and so on. Many large institutional pools of capital try to have managers who cover the spectrum of investment styles because different styles work better than others from time to time. If all styles are brought in under the investment umbrella, they hope not to underperform their peers or the broader market for any shortterm period. My problem with this approach is that it reinforces short-term thinking. If you know one style does best in the long run, maybe you shouldn't care about short-term performance comparisons. You also run the risk of building a portfolio that may look a lot like an index fund but with much higher costs. Better to go with an index fund and avoid all the management fees.

The typical money manager interview starts with a presentation of the manager's style and capabilities, all of which are, of course, excellent. Then comes the question-and-answer part of the meeting. The questions are usually the same, as are the answers. Money managers are not dummies. They know what the client wants to hear. The first question is, "Do you do your own research?" Absolutely. No one ever admits to reading brokerage firm research. Hundreds, if not thousands of security analysts at big brokerage firms are producing reports that no one reads although some of this research can be quite good. Second question: "Do you visit the companies you invest in?" Again, the answer is absolutely, and money managers usually claim that they will only talk to the CEO or the CFO. This is cause for concern: Given the number of money managers demanding lengthy, personal interviews with corporate CEOs and CFOs, I have to wonder who is running these businesses. One manager I interviewed claimed to make 250 company visits a year. That's one for every business day. Given travel time and the need for some sleep, when did this manager have time to read the annual reports? I have heard claims of 400 visits a year, and the all-time winner had a staff that made 4,000 visits. There isn't enough time to read 4,000 research reports in a given year. The third question institutional investors usually ask is, "Do you have a succession plan at your firm?" The client wants to know who will take over if something happens to the money manager. Every money manager has a good answer but concern for my well-being aside, unless I or any other money manager is 80 or 90, the interviewer should assume we plan on sticking around for a while. Limiting oneself to younger managers or only those managers with detailed succession plans would have ruled out Warren Buffett as a manager option. Still would. Lastly, the clients always want assurance they will have direct access to the manager. Why not just watch what the manager puts in your portfolio and leave them alone to do what you hired them to do in the first place?

I have a different set of criteria that you can apply to mutual funds as well as individual money managers.

First, does the manager have an investment approach and can explain it to you, or any layperson, in plain English, and has the manager applied it consistently over time? If you can't get direct face time with the manager, read all the shareholder letters and other promotional material published by the mutual fund for at least the past five years. Is it consistent in its approach to the market, or does the manager change horses midway through the race?

Second, what does the track record look like? Would you have been satisfied with the returns earned if you had been invested with them in the past? My preference is for at least 10 years of performance because that takes me through several market cycles. This is not always possible, but I would not go with less than a five-year record. It is also a good idea to note how volatile the returns have been. Some investors have a low tolerance for volatility, and you don't want to be scared out of the market just when stocks are their cheapest.

Third, whose record is it? Does the manager who produced the returns that you find acceptable, still run the fund? Whenever a fund changes managers, you can often expect a change in the management style unless the new manager apprenticed with the former manager for a long time. I interviewed a manager who presented a 25-year record of investing in growth stocks. The record was pretty good, not great. My biggest problem was that the manager was only 36 years old, so unless he began managing the fund when he was 11, much of the record was not relevant.

Fourth, what do the managers do with their own money? Are they invested in the fund alongside the money you intend to invest? Managers should eat their own cooking, as we say. They should be willing to assume the same investment risks they are asking you to assume by investing in their fund. There is something comforting about knowing that managers have their own money on the line. It keeps them from taking undue risks if they hit a rough patch in performance.

While this is not always a true indicator, I prefer funds where the individuals running the fund are also the owners of the investment management firm. If the firm is run by mutual fund marketers and salespeople, they may have more interest in gathering assets than managing the money well. The marketing types also tend to be shortterm focused, which puts pressure on the manager to make short-term investment decisions that may not be in your best interests. Money managers who also own their firm are freer to make long-term investment decisions, as only a client can fire them. These managers just have to convince their clients to stay around during some period when relative performance lags.

The secret to winning in the investment business is to pick good managers and stick with them.

Chapter Twenty

# You Can Lead a Horse to Water, But...

*You can't make it drink.*

By now, I should have made a good case for value investing. Let's recap a few key points: Value investing is straight forward; it does not require a superhuman set of brain cells. The average person can understand the logic of it all. Buy a dollar for 60 cents from some unsuspecting seller and wait until the person wants it back for a dollar. Most of the legends of the money management business pursued a value strategy, and they enjoyed or continue to enjoy careers spanning more years than the average age of many of today's hot money managers. Warren Buffett opened shop in 1957. He is still going strong 49 years later, which is the approximate age that some of the leading investment banks suggest their partners retire. Bill Ruane set his firm up in 1969 and remained active until just before he passed away in 2005. Walter Schloss started in 1954 and retired 49 years later at the age of 87. Others like John Neff, who ran the Windsor Fund; Jean-Marie Eveillard, of the SoGen Funds; and Bill Nygren, of the Oakmark Funds, had or continue to have long, successful careers. I have even been at it for 36 years, and I am still active full time. And two of my partners, John Spears and my brother Will, have been my partners for 31 years and 29 years, respectively. We have all shared the same investment philosophy—value investing. And we aren't going to change this far into the game. In a world where the average institutional account stays with a firm for three years, and the average mutual fund investor about the same, this is quite a record of achievement.

It has been my observation that value investing works long term, and that the strategy has never, to my knowledge, experienced any of the infamous blowups of racier, sexier investment styles. From time to time, you read about managers who recorded 100 percent losses in a matter of days or weeks. I've never seen a value manager on those lists.

There will always be managers who excel for a period of time although they do not follow a value investment philosophy. Some will even excel for fairly long periods. However, they are the exception. The true value adherents are in the majority of managers who have beaten the market over long periods.

So, if value investing is so smart, if it has been proven to be so successful, why do so few money managers or investors adhere to its principles? The answer is not intelligence. It is temperament. A whole field of academic study has emerged to analyze why investors, professional and individual, persist in making bad investment decisions despite empirical evidence that could guide them in the right direction. It is called behavioral psychology, and it was the topic of numerous seminars, conferences, books, and papers (some of which I cite in the bibliography) in the late 1990s and early 2000s.

Money management attracts some of the brightest and best educated people in the world. It does so because it is highly lucrative, and success can be measured daily at the close of the stock market. Mr. Market grades you on a daily basis rather than waiting for an annual salary review. The more IQ points you have, the more confident you become about your ability to be a successful money manager. Moreover, clients reinforce this point of view by seeking out experts who might have some secret ability to navigate the markets, much like the lost souls that trek to the Himalayas to find a guru who can reveal the secret of inner peace. All too often, money managers appear on the covers of financial magazines like movie stars on mountain bikes. They train physically so they will have the stamina to deal with turbulent markets. If only they would take a few hours to understand what successful money managers do, they could skip all the kickboxing and mountain climbing, or spend more time doing it as a leisure activity, if they find these sports enjoyable.

A herd instinct dominates the money management industry. If 95 percent of the money managers buy stock A and it goes down, there are no adverse consequences. After all, 95 percent of these smart managers were of the same opinion. However, if you were among the 5 percent who went against the herd and bought stock B, and it goes down, everyone says that you are a dummy. The reputational and career risk of being a contrarian is far greater than the risk of going with the flow. Value investing requires the ability to go against the herd—and to risk being called a dummy from time to time. In 1999, I received a letter from an investor asking, "How long are you going to stand around like ostriches with your heads in the sand waiting for the second coming of Elvis?" He said that there was value in technology and sent a list of stocks that on average were trading at 100 times earnings. Having seen cycles like this before, my partners and I stuck to our knitting with our low price-to-earnings and low-price-to-book value stocks. We held tight to the principles that had served us so well for decades. In the end, the boom went bust and our style was vindicated, and the stocks the shareholder had recommended were down about 90 percent a year later. Warren Buffett once said that returns using the value approach are "lumpy." There will be periods of underperformance to achieve higher long-term results. I know that; most of our investors know that. Nevertheless, it can be difficult for even committed value investors to remain steadfast in the face of so much hype and excitement.

Value investing also requires the mettle to buy those stocks that the majority of investors don't want to own. They have warts. They are out of favor. Of course, they are. Why else would they be cheap? When you go to cocktail parties and the talk turns to recent stock picks, one guy can say, "I bought Ionosphere Communications this morning at 10 and it closed at 12." Instantly, he is a genius. Forget that Ionosphere Communications has no sales and no earnings and is a disaster waiting to happen. You feel a bit foolish saying, "I bought ABC Ice Cream Corporation at half of book and 6 times earnings." You are greeted with a big yawn. Sex sells even in the stock market, and everyone wants to own the latest sexy issue. Value stocks are about as exciting as watching grass grow. But have you ever noticed just how much your grass grows in a week?

Most people seek immediate gratification in almost everything they do including investing. When most investors buy a stock, they expect it to go up immediately. If it doesn't, they sell it and buy something else. Value investors are more like farmers. They plant seeds and wait for the crops to grow. If the corn is a little late in starting because of cold weather, they don't tear up the fields and plant something else. No, they just sit back and wait patiently for the corn to pop out of the ground, confident that it will eventually sprout.

Overconfidence is another significant psychological flaw of most investors and money managers. People make changes in their portfolios because they are confident they are making a change for the better. Without that confidence, they would merely sit still. At a seminar during my twenty-fifth college reunion, I performed an experiment that psychologists have conducted on numerous occasions. In a group of people of approximately the same intelligence, everyone is asked to rate their investment skill relative to everyone else in the room on a scale of 1 to 10. We know the average has to be 5. Half will be smarter, half won't. However, the result of this experiment is consistently 7.5. It is just like Lake Wobegon, where everyone is above average. What else can explain the field of active money management when the reality is that only about 15 percent of money managers will beat an index over long periods of time. The managers and their clients must be confident they can beat the index despite empirical evidence that shows the vast majority will not. They all just believe that they will be the ones in the top 15 percent.

The same tendency toward overconfidence shows up in portfolio turnover rates. Again, investors sell stocks and buy other ones because they think the new stock will do better. Research has shown that overly confident investors trade more and make less. In a study of 100,000 trades by customers of Charles Schwab, the stocks that customers sold were 3.4 percent higher one year later than the stocks they bought. Investors who are less confident in their ability to make profitable decisions are more likely to sit still. The speed of trading is directly coordinated to the investors' individual confidence. In addition, investors who trade the most, tend to buy riskier stocks. They are looking for more action, confident that they can jump ship before it runs up on the rocks. To quote Blaise Pascal, "Most of men's problems arise from their inability to sit quietly and alone."

This rapid day trading is not confined to individual online brokerage customers seeking a Vegas fix. Many professionals are just as prone to the overconfidence syndrome. Jason Zweig, of *Money* magazine, reported in a Peter Bernstein newsletter that in 1959 the average mutual fund had a portfolio turnover rate of 16.4 percent and the average holding period for a stock was six years. Today, the turnover rate is well over 100 percent and still heading higher. Confidence is partly to blame, but peer group pressures also encourage this behavior. The investment world now equates activity with intelligence. If you are a portfolio manager, you are paid to act. You should be aware that selling Pfizer today and buying Johnson & Johnson is a smart move. Merely sitting with a portfolio of good stocks you have carefully researched and selected is not enough. Sooner or later, someone upstairs will notice a lack of activity in your portfolio and will ask why. You could say you just happen to prefer the stocks you own to the others out there, but that sounds wimpy. It implies a lack of market savvy and a lot of indecisiveness. So you trade in a futile effort to improve returns.

Everyone knows that stock markets go up and they go down. Fortunately, the long-term trend is up. Otherwise, who needs stocks? Long term, everyone says their goal is to beat the market, and nearly all investors claim that they are conservative. In the short term, however, the investors' view may vary. When markets are rising, they want to do better than the market. When markets are falling, they want to lose less than the market. In rising markets, many investors throw caution to the wind in an effort to beat a rising market. In declining markets, many investors head for the exits to conserve their net worth. Winning on both sides of the stock market cycle is no small feat. However, in the 31 years from 1975 through 2005, the S&P 500 has risen more than 20 percent in 12 of 31 years, nearly 39 percent of the time. If you just did as good or nearly as good as the market in those years, you should be happy. In the not-so-good years, the S&P 500 either lost money or rose at a rate less than half its 31-year averaged compounded rate of return of 13.5 percent. Good long-term performance results from beating the market in the bad times. Caution should not be seasonal. One should not rediscover caution when markets are falling and forget about it when they are rising. Maintaining a steady state of mind, whether we are in good times or bad, is the key to successful long-term investing.

Many smart and deservedly respected market observers advise investors that beating the market is a formidable task. Whether it is because advisory fees and transaction costs are too great a burden to overcome, or investors and money managers alike make badly timed decisions, beating the market is almost impossible. They still counsel investors to stay in stocks but to do it through index funds. While it is true that long-term index funds will beat most money managers, 85 percent by some estimates, index funds are not a silver bullet. The S&P 500 year-end peak in 1928 was 24.35. Following the crash of 1929 and the Great Depression, it did not reach that level again until 1952, a span of 24 years. (Dividends were pretty generous over that period, so investors with dividends included would have recouped their 1928 investment a number of years earlier.) Following the 1972 year-end peak for the S&P 500, it took 5 years for investors to be whole with dividends reinvested. And from the year-end 1999 peak, through the end of 2005, 6 long years, the S&P 500 with dividends reinvested is still 7 percent below its December 31, 1999, value. Patience is a virtue, but waiting 5, 6, or 20 years just to get your money back is a stretch.

My own observation of value managers is that they tend not to go through such long performance droughts. Why? Even indexes can be victims of bubbles. The three periods cited previously all followed periods of excess in the market: the roaring twenties, the Nifty-Fifty period of the early 1970s, and the tech bubble of the late 1990s. In all cases, the excesses of a relatively small number of hot stocks distorted the performance of the S&P 500. Most recently, in 1999, the technology sector of the S&P 500 accounted for more than 30 percent of the index versus a historic average of about 15 or 16 percent. At certain times, an index is not a conservative investment.

Jeremy Seigel, the renowned finance professor at the Wharton School of the

University of Pennsylvania, has also been an advocate of indexing. In his book, *The Future for Investors,* he made the case for customized indexes, which are now possible. He found that indexes that exclude the highest P/E stocks and include some smaller and mid-cap stocks did far better than the broader index. In essence, value counts. An index that emphasizes lower P/E value stocks does better. I could have told him that years ago.

Being a contrarian, which true value investors are, is not easy. Lots of pressures are working against you. The wild swings of momentum and growth investing tend to subject investors to more thrills, and ultimately more spills, than the value approach. Value investing is more like a long trip to a pleasant destination than a ride on a roller coaster.

# Chapter Twenty-One

# Stick to Your Guns

Years of practical experience have taught me that the patient exercise of value investing principles works, and works well. My partners and I have all had long, successful careers and have done very well for ourselves and our investors using the techniques outlined in this book, as have numerous other value devotees. In fact, I don't know a single poor value manager who has been in the business more than 10 years. Value investing requires more effort than brains, and a lot of patience. It is more grunt work than rocket science. But over time, investors should continue to be rewarded for buying stocks on the cheap.

Through the years, there have been changes in the methods of finding value stocks, and in the criteria that define value. When Ben Graham began managing money in the late 1920s, there were no databases, there was no Internet. The information age had not arrived. Back then, the search for undervalued stocks meant poring through the Moody's and Standard & Poor's tomes for stocks that fit the value criteria. Now, you can accomplish this with the click of a mouse. We can access almost all the data we need off a CD-ROM or our Bloomberg terminals. We no longer have to run around gathering 10k reports or annual shareholder letters. They are all right there on the Internet for us to access for U.S. and non-U.S. stocks all over the world.

Trading has changed as well. For the most part, trading is now done electronically with no effort at all. We can trade stocks in Tokyo or London just as easily as we can in New York. When we need to discuss a stock or enter orders, we can communicate from the office or anywhere else we may be via cell phone or wireless laptop computers.

However, this change has been relatively recent. For 60 years, from the days when Benjamin Graham went into the business in the late 1920s beyond when I started in 1969, the improvements in communication, the way people traded stocks, and the availability of information remained much the same. We had touchtone phones and direct lines, but not much else. I can remember buying the firm's first calculator. It was clunky and heavy, and cost a lot even by today's standards, but it did have a new invention called *memory.* There was no NASDAQ Stock Market in 1969. Over-the-counter stocks were still listed on the Pink Sheets and you had to call brokers for quotes. Everything was recorded on paper, and stock certificates were still delivered by runners.

Ben Graham pored over Moody's and Standard & Poor's manuals and so did I. The first database of company filings appeared in the mid-1970s from a firm named Compustat. In the beginning, we would call Compustat, tell them the criteria we wanted them to use in screening stocks, and they would send us a tape we could run on our own computer. We had a computer by then, but the term *desktop* had not yet come into being. We now take for granted the explosion in information availability that has taken place in the past 10 or 15 years and wonder how anyone functioned before e-mail, Windows, and Google.

Just as the access to information and the methods of trading stocks have changed in the past two decades, so have the criteria for value changed. One of my first jobs when I began my career in 1969 was looking through the Standard & Poor's monthly stock guide for stocks selling below net current assets. This was a primary source of cheap stocks in those days. The method had been pioneered by Graham and was very successful. Generally, we were buying stocks that sold for less than their liquidation value. Back then, manufacturing companies pretty much dominated the U.S. economy as they had for decades.

As the U.S. economy grew in the 1960s, 1970s, and 1980s, it began to move away from the heavy industrial manufacturing companies such as steel and textiles. Consumer product companies and service companies became more a part of the landscape. These companies needed less physical assets to produce profits, and their tangible book values were less meaningful as a measure of value. Many value investors had to adapt and began to look more closely at earnings-based models of valuation. Radio and television stations and newspapers were examples of businesses that could generate enormous earnings with little in the way of physical assets and thus had fairly low tangible book value. The ability to learn new ways to look at value allows you to make some profitable investments that you might well have overlooked had you not adapted with the times.

Along the way I also learned that there was a great deal of money to be made buying companies that could grow their earnings at a faster rate than the old industrial type companies. I believe it was Warren Buffett who made the statement that growth and value are joined at the hip. The difference between growth and value was mostly a question of price. I paid a little more than I might have in the old days of just buying stocks based on book value but found great bargains like American

Express, Johnson & Johnson, and Capital Cities Broadcasting. Companies like these were able, and in many cases still are able, to grow at rates significantly greater than the economy overall and were worth a higher multiple of earnings than a basic manufacturing business.

In the mid-1980s, the leveraged buyout business was born. The U.S. economy was emerging from a period of high inflation and high interest rates. Inflation had increased the value of the assets of many companies. For example, if ABC Ice Cream had built a new factory 5 years ago for $10 million and was depreciating it over a 10-year period, it would have been written down to $5 million on ABC's books. However, after 5 years of inflation, it might cost $15 million to replace that factory. Its value is understated on the company's books. Using the factory as collateral, the company might have been able to borrow 60 percent of its current value, or $9 million. This is what LBO firms did with all sorts of assets in the 1980s. They would borrow against a company's assets to finance the purchase of the company.

Additionally, the record high interest rates of the late 1970s and early 1980s drove stock prices to their lowest levels in decades. The price-to-earnings ratio of the Standard & Poor's 500 was in the single digits. With long-term Treasury bonds yielding 14 percent, who needed to own stocks? The combination of significant undervalued collateral and low P/E ratios made many companies ripe for acquisition at very low prices. A typical deal in the mid-1980s might be done at only 4.5 times pretax earnings. Today, that number is more in the range of 9 to 12 times pretax earnings. This period was a once-in-a-lifetime opportunity to buy companies at record cheap prices in terms of both assets and earnings.

I try to track as many acquisitions as I can, noting the price in relation to book value and pretax earnings. By doing so, I can construct a model of acquisition values. I use this model to screen for companies that are selling in the stock market at a significant discount to what an LBO group might pay. The LBO model gave me one more way of defining "cheap." I call it the *appraisal method.* I still use low price-to-book value ratios and low P/E ratios to search for undervalued stocks, but I have added the appraisal method as a third leg of my value stool. If there is another way to find stocks that sell for far less than they are worth, I like to take advantage of it.

The methods and criteria have changed over the years, and they will evolve further with the march of time and inevitable change. What is important is that the principles have not changed. The basic idea of buying stocks for less than they are worth and selling them as they approach their true worth is at the heart of value investing. On balance, value investing is easier than other forms of investing. It is not necessary to spend eight hours a day glued to a screen trading frenetically in and out of stocks. By paying attention to the basic principle of buying below intrinsic value with a margin of safety and exercising patience, investors will find that the value approach continues to offer investors the best way to beat the stock market indexes and increase wealth over time.

Patience is sometimes the hardest part of using the value approach. When I find a stock that sells for 50 percent of what I have determined it is worth, my job is basically done. Now it is up to the stock. It may move up toward its real worth today, next week, or next year. It may trade sideways for five years and then quadruple in price. There is simply no way to know when a particular stock will appreciate, or if, in fact, it will. There will be periods when the value approach will underperform other strategies, and that can be frustrating. Perhaps even more frustrating are those times when the overall market has risen to such high levels that we are unable to find many stocks that meet our criteria for sound investing. It is sometimes tempting to give in and perhaps relax one criterion just a bit, or chase down some of the hot money stocks that seem to go up forever. But, just about the time that value investors throw in the towel and begin to chase performance is when the hot stocks get ice cold.

Benjamin Graham laid out the basic concepts of the value approach to investing many decades ago. Like Graham, I have no faith in my ability, or in the ability of most others, to predict the direction of stock prices over the short term. I do not believe that many people can detect which technology stock will be the next Microsoft or which ones will bomb. What I do know is that owning a diversified portfolio of stocks that meets the standards of a margin of safety and are cheap, based on one or more valuation methods, has proven to be a sound way to invest my money. I have no reason to believe it will not continue to be so.

# Don't Take My Word for It

I don't expect you to simply take my word for the continued success of the value method of investing. I admit to bias; value is how I make my living. Fortunately, there exists independent confirmation by many academics and scholars who have relentlessly studied what does and what does not work in the stock market. The following is a quick review of the major studies and their findings.

## U.S. Stocks

One of the first studies done on PE ratios and performance was authored by Professor Sanjoy Basu of McMaster University. In "Investment Performance of Common Stocks in Relation to Their Price Earnings Ratios" he looked at stocks listed on the New York Stock exchange from 1957 to 1971. For each year he divided all the listed stocks into five equal groups or quintiles and examined their future performance. He found that value stocks far outperformed their growth peers with a hypothetical $1 million investment growing to more than twice what the higher PE stocks would have achieved.

In his study "Decile Portfolios of the New York Stock Exchange, 1967–1985," Yale professor Roger Ibbotson ranked all the stocks in 10 equally weighted groups (deciles) according to their P/E ratios. He examined all listed stocks from 1966 to 1984 and found that the cheaper, less popular stocks gave far greater returns. In fact, $1 invested in the cheapest stocks grew to over six times as much as the highest P/E ratio companies and twice as much as those in the middle of the pack. He also looked at how stocks selling at very low multiples of book value compared with growth stocks selling at much higher multiples of asset value. He sorted all the stocks on the New York Stock Exchange (NYSE) into deciles (groupings of 10) for each year and compared the performance of each group. He looked at stocks from 1967 to 1984 and found that stocks priced very low compared to book value outperformed the glamorous names by better than two to one and the market as a whole by better than 75 percent.

One of my favorite studies that I often refer to when discussing the merits of the value versus growth approach to investing was done by Josef Lakonishok, Robert Vishney, and Andrei Shliefer entitled "Contrarion Investment, Extrapolation and Risk." It ranks all the stocks on both the New York and American Stock Exchanges by P/E ratio in deciles. Each portfolio was held for five years and then sold. They found that across the range of five-year holding periods, the low P/E stocks offered almost twice as much return. Imagine—twice as much in as short a time as five years! They also ranked stocks by price-to-book ratio, also in deciles, and held them for five years. They examined stock prices from 1968 to 1990. Once again, those selling cheapest when compared to book value outperformed by a very wide margin, almost three times the more glamorous stocks, over the five-year holding period. In this same study, they found that the low price-to-book stocks outperformed growth selection in 73 percent of one-year holding periods, 90 percent of three-year, and 100 percent of the five-year holding periods.

One of the most exhaustive examinations of the performance of value stocks was done by Richard Thaler and Werner FM De Bondt, then professors at the University of Wisconsin and Cornell University, respectively. In a 1985 edition of the *Journal of Finance* they published a paper, "Does the Stock Market Overreact?" that looked at the idea of buying stocks that had gone bump in the night and performed poorly against those that had shone in the sun and performed the best. They examined stock prices starting in December 1932 through 1977, a period covering 46 market years. They looked at the 35 stocks on the New York Stock Exchange that performed the worst over the prior five years against the 35 listed stocks that had been the brightest stars. They compared the results of investing in each basket with an index made up of an equally weighted portfolio of all stocks on the NYSE. They found that, on average, over the next 17 months, the worst stocks gained about 17 percent more than the index, and the bright stars of the past faded quickly returning about 6 percent *less* than the index over the time period. They also studied holding the portfolios of stocks over three years and found that the prior "bad" stocks continued to far outperform the best past performers. In 1987, Werner FM De Bondt and Richard Thaler further sorted stocks into quintiles (groupings of 20) in their research paper "Further Evidence on Investor Overreaction and Stock Market Seasonality" and found that the stocks selling below book value outperformed the market by more than 40 percent, or almost 9 percent a year.

In a study that compared PE ratios within industry groups, Professors David Goodman and John Peavy of Southern Methodist University ranked stocks within industry groups across more than 100 different industries according to PE ratios. They sorted all the different groups into quintiles and found that even within more specific groupings, the stocks with lower price-to-earnings ratios far outperformed the higher priced stocks. A dollar invested in the bottom quintile of each group, rebalanced annually, grew to over 12 times the highest P/E group and more than twice those with the second lowest P/E ratios.

In their 1992 study "The Cross Section of Expected Stock Returns," Eugene Fama and Kenneth French examined all nonfinancial stocks included in the Center for Research in Security Prices files, perhaps the most comprehensive database of stock prices. Their study covered the period from 1963 to 1990. They used deciles of stocks ranked according to price-to-book value. The lowest price-to-book value stocks returned almost three times as much as the highest over the 27-year time period. They also looked at holding the portfolios of stocks over three years and found that the prior "bad" stocks continued to far outperform the best past performers.

# Global Stocks

As discussed, stocks that have value characteristics perform well in and outside the United States. It was a delight to serendipitously stumble on some value opportunities in Japan when we found insurance companies selling for onethird of book value in the 1980s, but independent research confirms that all around the globe buying stocks selling below book value is a sound idea.

I found of particular interest a study done by Mario Levis, a professor at the School of Management, University of Bath in the United Kingdom, that looked at all the stocks in the London Share database. He looked at stocks from 1961 to 1985 and sorted them into quintiles. Once again, the lower P/E ratio stocks outperformed more exciting growth companies by an extraordinary margin. Over that time period, $1 invested in the lowest price-to-earnings ratio group returned more than five times the highest ratio stocks and double that of those in group two. Performance was three times as high as the companies in the middle group of P/E levels.

In a Morgan Stanley research paper titled "Ben Graham Would Be Proud," Barton Biggs examined the return for low price-to-book value investing around the world. About 80 percent of the stocks in the study were outside the United States and, once again, the cheap stocks outperformed the more expensive as well as the world market indexes. Nobel Prize winner William Sharpe looked at stocks in Germany, France, Switzerland, the United Kingdom, the United States, and Japan in his *Financial Analysts Journal* article in 1993 titled "International Value and Growth Stocks." He examined stocks in the S&P 500 in the United States and stocks included in the Morgan Stanley Capital International Index for the other nations. He ranked the stocks every six months. The top 50 percent of stocks in price-to-book value were the growth portfolio, and the 50 percent that sold lowest compared with asset value were the value portfolio. From 1981 through 1992, the value stocks outperformed the growth stocks in each and every country by a substantial margin.

# Losers to Winners

Academic research also supports many value investing techniques. James Porterba of the Massachusetts Institute of Technology and Lawrence Summers of Harvard (who later went on to become Secretary of the Treasury and the controversial president of Harvard) in March 1998 published a paper entitled "Mean Reversion in Stock Prices, Evidence and Implications." They looked at monthly stock prices on the NYSE from 1926 to 1985 to determine if large price increases or decreases were followed by reversals or continued in the original direction. They found that current high investment returns tended to be followed by lower returns, and low investment returns tended to lead to higher performance. In total, they examined stock price reactions in 17 nations including the United States, the United Kingdom, Switzerland, Canada, Japan, Belgium, and the Netherlands. They found that stock prices tended to act the same all over the globe. Today's worst stocks became tomorrow's best, and the darlings of the day becoming the spinsters of the next day.

# Insider Buying

In "What Has Worked in Investing," a paper authored by Tweedy, Browne, we examined several key studies that show the tremendous outperformance of stocks with insider buying. We looked at five key studies that showed that stocks with insider buying outperformed the stock market by at least a two-to-one margin. We also looked at several studies that examined insider buying in countries around the world and found that insider buying was predictive of higher returns on a global basis as well. Only a few countries outside the United States require insiders to report transactions, so the information is not as useful.

Fortunately, the field of academic research into financial markets is ongoing and prolific. Many papers have looked at the relationship between insider buying and future returns. One such study by Thomas George and Nejat Seyhun of the University of Michigan looked at over 1 million transactions over a 21-year period. They found that stocks with insider buying outperformed the market by over 6 percent over the next 12 months. The conclusions shared by Professor Seyhun and myself are further borne out in a study by Fuller Thaler Asset Management entitled "Extrapolation Bias, Insider Trading." In 2001, Andrew Metrick of the Wharton School, Leslie Jeng of Boston University, and Richard Zeckhauser of Harvard released their paper "Estimating the Returns to Insider Trading, a Performance Evaluation Perspective" that confirmed these findings. They looked at insider activity and stock prices from 1975 to 1996 and found that those companies with insiders buying stock outperformed the overall stock market by about the same 6 percent. A 2003 paper by Joseph Piotroski and Darrell Roulstone of the University of Chicago found that insider buying signaled that earnings and cash flow would improve over the next 12 months, leading to a higher stock price. They looked at stocks selling at low earnings multiples or below book value between 1984 and

1995 and found that companies with these characteristics with heavy buying by insiders dramatically and substantially outperformed the market. They also found that those with high multiples and insider selling tended to underperform by a wide margin.

The same held true for companies that bought back stock. One of the first studies into the effect of stock buybacks was done in a *Fortune* magazine article by Carol Loomis in 1985. She looked at all the stocks in the Value Line universe from 1974 to 1983 and found that companies that bought back stock earned 50 percent more annually than those that did not. A study by University of Illinois professors David Ikenberry and Josef Lakonishok in 1994 looked at companies that bought back stock from 1980 to 1990 and found that over the next four years they outperformed the market by 12.1 percent. For those companies that had other value traits selling at low prices to earnings or book value the professors found that the outperformance was over 45 percent.

Another study done by Professor Ikenberry, with Konan Chan and Inmoo Lee, found that companies that bought back stock between 1980 and 1996 averaged 6 percent more than the market over 12 months and 23 percent over four years. In his most recent study released in 2005, Ikenberry looked at stock buybacks by companies with good earnings and low valuations. He found that, between 1980 and 2000, companies that repurchased stock outperformed by better than 35 percent over four years.

# The Latest Look

Lest you think that we rely only on older studies to prove the worth of buying stocks with low prices when compared to earnings, a study from the Brandes Institute, a part of Brandes Asset Management, a venerable value firm, repeated the work of Lakonishok, Vishney, and Shliefer on U.S. stocks, updated it through 2004, and also conducted a similar study of international stocks. Its research showed that the low PE ratio stocks, when tested from 1969 all the way through 2002, have far outperformed the higher priced growth issues. In addition, Professor Lakonishok, along with Louis Chen at the University of Illinois, updated his studies through the year 2002 and found that the value strategy of buying stocks cheaply based on earnings continued to vastly outperform other stocks. They also released a study that examined returns on U.S. stocks from 1986 through 2002. They looked at stocks that they called *falling knives,* a play on the old Wall Street adage of never trying to catch a falling knife. They defined falling knives as stocks that had fallen 60 percent in price over the prior 12 months. They found that although these stocks did indeed represent a risky proposition with a bankruptcy and failure rate four times that of the market as a whole, as a group they far outperformed the market over one-, two-, and three-year holding periods. Not surprisingly they found that the larger the market capitalization of the company, the higher the outperformance and the less the chance of corporate failure. As one of the chief tenets of our value investing approach is to always maintain a margin of safety, the likelihood of buying into an undercapitalized or poorly financed falling knife would seem to be lessened, giving us an opportunity for further outperformance of the market averages. The Brandes Institute updated this work and took a global look at falling knives in a 2004 paper titled "Falling Knives Around the World," examining stocks from around the world from 1980 to 2003. As with the previous study, it looked at companies with a market capitalization of over $100 million that had fallen 60 percent in price after the price collapse. Not only did the falling knives in the United States continue to show marked outperformance over the market as a whole, this outperformance held true around the globe.

Value investing works. It has worked in actual investing and it is confirmed by many research studies.

# Bibliography

"Ben Graham Would Be Proud," Morgan Stanley & Co., April 1991, Barton M. Biggs.

"Contrarian Investment Extrapolation and Risk, National Bureau of Economic Research," May 1993, Josef Lakonishok, Robert Vishney, and Andrei Shleifer.

"The Cross Section of Expected Stock Returns," University of Chicago, January 1992, Eugene Fama and Kenneth French.

"Currency and Hedging: The Longer Term Perspective," Brandes Institute, November 2005.

"Decile Portfolios of the New York Stock Exchange, 1967–85," Yale School of Management, 1986, Roger Ibbotson.

"Does the Stock Market Overreact?" *Journal of Finance,* July 1985, Werner FM De Bondt and Richard Thaler.

"Do Insider Trades Reflect Both Contrarian Beliefs and Superior Knowledge about Future Cash Flow Realizations?" *Journal of Accounting and Economics,* 2005, Joseph D. Piotroski, Darren T. Roulstone.

"Economic Sources of Gain in Stock Repurchases," University of Illinois, 1998, Konan Chan, David Ikenberry, and Inmoo Lee.

"Estimating the Returns to Insider Trading, A Performance Evaluation Perspective," *Review of Economics and Statistics,* 1994, Andrew Metrick, Leslie Jeng, and Richard Zeckhauser.

"Extensive Insider Buying as an Indicator of Near Term Stock Prices," Ohio State University, 1966, Gary Glass.

"Extrapolation Bias, Insider Trading," 1994, Fuller Thaler Asset Management.

"Falling Knives around the World," Brandes Institute, August 2004.

"The Forecasting Properties of Insider Transactions," Michigan State University, 1964, Donald Rogoff.

"Further Evidence on Investor Overreaction and Stock Market Seasonality," *Journal of Finance,* July 1987, Werner FM De Bondt and Richard Thaler.

*The Future for Investors: Why the Tried and True Triumph Over the Bold and New,* Jeremy Siegel, McGraw-Hill, 2005.

*Hyper Profits,* Doubleday and Company, 1985, David Goodman and John Peavy III.

"International Value and Growth Stock Returns," *Financial Analysts Journal,* January/February 1993, William Sharpe, Carlo Capaul, and Ian Rowley.

"Investment Performance of Common Stocks in Relation to Their Price Earnings Ratios: A Test of the Efficient Market Hypothesis," *Journal of Finance,* June 1977, Sanjoy Basu.

"Market Efficiency and Insider Trading," University of Michigan, 1994, Njat Sayhun and Thomas George.

"Market Size, PE Ratios, Dividend Yield and Share Price," University of Bath, United Kingdom, 1989, Mario Levis.

"Market Underreaction to Open Market Share Repurchases," 1994, *Journal of Financial Economics,* David Ikenberry and Josef Lakonishok.

"Mean Reversion in Stock Prices, Evidence and Implications," March 1988, Lawrence Summers and James Porterba.

"Quantitative Application for Research Analysts," Investing Worldwide II, Association for Investment Management and Research, 1991, John Chisolm.

"Searching for Rational Investors in a Perfect Storm," Louis Lowenstein, Columbia University, 2004.

"Special Information and Insider Trading, Portland College, 1968," *Journal of Business,* Jaffrey Jaffe.

*Stocks for the Long Run,* 3rd edition, Jeremy Siegel, McGraw-Hill, 2002.

"Time in the Market: A Buy-and-Hold Strategy Makes Sense for Long-Term Investing," American Century Investments, 2006.

"Value Investing and Falling Knives," The Brandes Institute, July 2003.

"The Value of Information: Inferences from the Profitability of Insider Trading," *Journal of Financial and Quantitative Analysis,* September 1979, Jerome Baesal and Garry Stein.

"Value versus Glamour, Updated and Expanded," Brandes Institute, October 2005.

"The Velocity of Learning and the Future of Active Management," Jason Zweig, *Economic and Portfolio Strategy,* February 1, 1999.

# Front Cover Flap

Do you care about your money? Then spend a little time with Christopher Browne to understand what investing is all about so you can do a better job of investing.

There are many ways to make money in today's market, but the one strategy that has truly proven itself over the years is value investing. Value investing consists of buying the stock of companies that trade for less than their intrinsic value to profit from their long-term performance. Value investing works. It has produced superior investment results to any other strategy. Best of all, it is easy to understand. As Warren Buffett has said, no more than 125 IQ points are needed. Any more and they are wasted.

Author Christopher Browne has been a part of Tweedy, Browne Company—the oldest value investing firm on Wall Street, which has counted Benjamin Graham among its clients—for more than thirty years, and over the course of his career, he has successfully followed the value approach to investment management, buying bargain stocks around the world.

Now, with *The Little Book of Value Investing,* he translates this wealth-building strategy in a way that any investor can understand and apply to investing all over the globe. You will learn how to buy stocks like steaks—on sale—no matter where they are sold; how to put your money to work like a banker; and how to buy $1 for 66 cents. Browne's ideas can help prevent you from losing money by spotting false bargains. Most importantly, he clearly illuminates the first rule of investing: don't lose money.

The beauty of value investing is its logical simplicity. Within these pages, high-caliber value manager Christopher Browne illustrates how to identify the "sales flyers," the market offers to profit, while avoiding bubbles and manias. This little book is a treasure trove of insight. In addition to teaching you how to uncover value stocks, you'll also learn how to:

- Give the companies you invest in a physical

- Send your stocks to the Mayo Clinic for a checkup with a sixteen-point checklist
- Find a specialist
- Stay the course and stay away from fleeting fads

Written in a straightforward and engaging manner, *The Little Book of Value Investing* will help you to understand and implement one of the most effective investment strategies ever created.

# Back Cover Flap

CHRISTOPHER H. BROWNE is a Managing Director of Tweedy, Browne Company LLC and is a member of the firm's management committee. He is also President of the Tweedy, Browne Funds, a mutual fund group. Browne is a graduate of the University of Pennsylvania where he serves as a Charter (Life) Trustee. At Penn, he established the Browne Center for International Politics, and the Browne Distinguished Professorships in the School of Arts and Sciences. Mr. Browne served on the faculty advisory committee of Harvard's John F. Kennedy School of Government program in investment decisions and behavioral finance. He is a trustee of Guild Hall, a regional arts and education center in East Hampton, New York, and of the Long Island Chapter of The Nature Conservancy. Mr. Browne is also a trustee of The Rockefeller University and a member of its executive and investment committees.

# Back Cover Material

LITTLE BOOK
BIG PROFITS™

*"In value investing, you cannot do better."*
—Roger Lowenstein

*"Chris Browne is one of the best value investors in the world. What he has to say is always worth paying attention to."*
—Barton M. Biggs, Traxis Partners, and author, *Hedgehogging*

*"Legendary value investor Chris Browne derived his skills from Ben Graham and Warren Buffett. His helpful book, filled with common sense and uncommon insights, distills his four decades of experience into a set of guidelines that will make any investor more effective."*
—Byron R. Wien, Pequot Capital Management

*"Forget Wall Street. It's a promotion machine. Forget almost all books on*

*investing. They won't help you. But this book will. Chris Browne makes sense."*
—Jean-Marie Eveillard, former portfolio manager, First Eagle Funds

*"Brilliant value investor Chris Browne uses this gem of a book to explain how value investing works, how to understand value in a stock, how to use accounting information on domestic and foreign firms to your advantage, and how to allocate your (hopefully growing!) portfolio over time."*
—Glenn Hubbard, Dean and Russell L. Carson Professor of Finance and Economics, Columbia Business School

www.ingramcontent.com/pod-product-compliance
Lightning Source LLC
Chambersburg PA
CBHW061149220326
41599CB00025B/4412